Building an Empathy-Based Classroom

A Teacher's Survival Guide

Ken Klieman

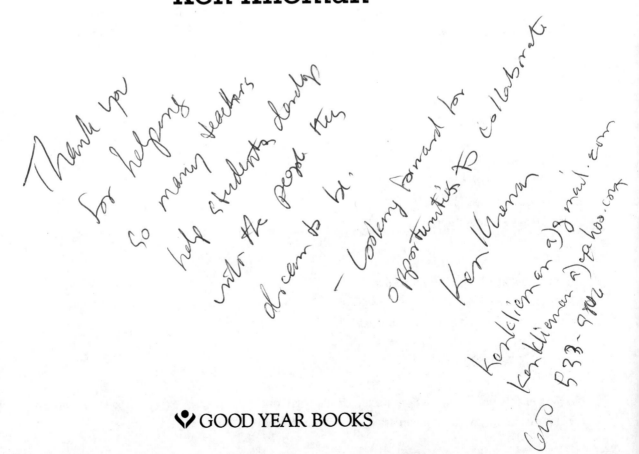

❤ GOOD YEAR BOOKS

Dedication

This book is dedicated to the teachers who have the courage to "think beyond yourself" and act on their best intentions for kindness, inclusivity and the community good. It is more important to help build the person than the student.

Acknowledgements

This book would not be possible if it wasn't for the preeminent role model I could ever imagine learning from for living a values driven, empathic life – my wife and life partner, Diane Friedlaender. Thank you for helping me to be a better man than I could ever be on my own.

The ideals of compassion and grace, which are the constant underpinnings of this book, were first taught to me by my mother, Charlotte Klieman. Thank you.

Thank you to my three courageous children, Zach, Miles, and Josephina. Your patience, friendship, and love buttress me throughout all of my days.

Thank you to my friends and family for your encouragement and patience with me.

Finally, students don't remember content as much as they remember adults who make the extra effort to care, model inclusivity and kindness. I have been fortunate to have two such role models in my life: Maybelline Truesdell, and Kathy Kline. Thank you for investing your love in me so I can pass it along to thousands of others.

❤ GOOD YEAR BOOKS

Our titles are available for most basic curriculum subjects plus many enrichment areas. For information on other Good Year Books and to place orders, contact your local bookseller or educational dealer, or visit our website at www.goodyearbooks.com. For a complete catalog, please contact:

Good Year Books
A Division of Social Studies School Service
10200 Jefferson Boulevard
Culver City, CA 90232-0802

(800) 421-4246

Book layout by A.R. Harter
Editor: Aarya Chevaillier

Table of Contents

Foreword by Ann Lieberman

ANYBODY who has been a teacher or a teacher educator will be thrilled to read Ken Klieman's book *Building an Empathy-Based Classroom: A Teacher's Survival Guide*. All readers will wonder why this book wasn't written ages ago. As someone who taught sixth grade with forty-six kids in my first year of teaching over fifty years ago, I can still remember and feel the angst, confusion, excitement, need to control, and nightmares. Where was Ken Klieman when I needed him?

The answer is that years later, he was learning to teach himself and thinking hard about how to answer and solve the myriad questions and conundrums that new teachers find themselves facing— most often with no one there to help.

This is not just a book for first year teachers, but for anyone who considers themselves a learning teacher trying to get a hold of the curriculum, the students, the institutional and changing imperatives, as well as their own sense of self. Klieman gently and sensitively nurtures our intellect, our understanding, and our soul by painstakingly describing the complexities of teaching, as they often occur without warning, sometimes in the midst of the best intentions. And he offers more than a helping hand! After reading the book I realized that only a teacher could have written this kind of a book—a teacher who had lived the many experiences over time—a teacher who could gather his wisdom to reach out to his fellow colleagues—a teacher who continues to learn, and who now mentors others as they face what it means to teach and how to solve the complexities of teaching in a changing educational climate.

Klieman walks us through the life of a teacher, starting with the beginning of school. How do you start your class on the right foot?

How should you organize the activities on day one? How do you make the classroom important, and at the same time let the students know they are important members of this classroom culture and must help in making it work? And he lovingly provides us with numerous ways to answer the questions that inevitably arise during the first day of school (after a no doubt sleepless night).

My favorite chapter is the one on "Giving Praise to Individuals or the Entire Class" in which Klieman mentors us on how to keep the class moving, engaged, and humming. After struggling with trying to differentiate instruction, learning how to participate in staff meetings, dealing with students who need extra help, and understanding and reaching out to parents, we finally feel that we are getting at what it means to teach. And Klieman is there, helping us understand how to think about both innovating and creating norms in the classroom that keep both teacher and students wanting to not only be in class, but to participate fully in a culture in the making.

Three values are constant in the book: Klieman's empathy for novice teachers, mentoring examples that grow out of practice, and his understanding that learning to teach never stops. What makes this book so good is that these values comprise its strong foundation.

The tone is intelligent, friendly, and caring; the examples for each topic are rooted in the real world of teaching practice; and Klieman reminds us that learning to teach is a lifetime affair, and so to always be open to new experiences, new learning, and new personal observations and insights.

By making school and classroom problems accessible, and in some ways solvable, we learn to make teaching a reflective practice. Klieman keeps us from harboring all the struggle of learning to teach as solely a personal problem. Many problems are inevitable, describable, and solvable! And now we have a mentor beside us, nurturing us to think about a variety of options, actions, and attitudes that can help us get better and better. We learn to try things, to take risks, and to not get defeated, but rather to continue to grow, learn, and even flower. This kind of support written by a teacher for teachers was worth waiting for!

Ann Lieberman,
Senior Scholar at Stanford University and
emeritus professor from Teachers College, Columbia University.

How to Use This Book

OVER the past twenty years of teaching middle school, I have been humbled many times because of a lack of foresight. Just like millions of other teachers, I have spent thousands of hours of introspection dissecting the intricacies of school relationships, and school cultures. I never think that I have all of the answers. But I have been able to learn from some true leaders in education about how to infuse more promise, collaboration and action to fulfill our best intentions for our schools.

This book is an attempt to act as an informed mentor for beginning teachers by following the format of the popular "Choose Your Own Adventure" book series. Readers will be able to explore multiple outcomes centered on specific aspects of teaching. It is the "Sim Life" for teachers, in book form.

Teachers struggle with all kinds of problems—all at once—and we often feel alone. Sometimes the problems come so thick and fast, that we don't even have time enough to articulate them. Little has been written about these problems and possibilities of teaching, in part because they need to come from practice. By providing a veteran perspective, all teachers can explore the outcome of their ideas in a quick, entertaining, exploratory format. Since *Building an Empathy-Based Classroom* will enable the reader to pursue the path of their own curiosity throughout the book, it provides a unique, simulated journey of learning through experience that has never been done before in the vast canon of teacher education manuals.

The reality is that none of us will ever be fully loved by every student. Teaching is a slow transformative marathon, for our students and for ourselves. To be a life-long, effective educator is to be someone who is never satisfied with getting by. The process of pursuing perfection is perfection itself. The more we embrace the chaos of being open to constant improvement, the less scary life as a teacher becomes.

A longitudinal perspective is the key element. The overarching focus for the year should be on fostering students' independence, both socially and academically. Being able to predict outcomes is the measure of mastery. Specifically, the consistency and routine in our classrooms ought to enable our students to perfect their work habits, academic skills, and positive social habits. To empower students to reach their own academic destinies, we need to model, model, and model some more. Hence the first part of a year should be more teacher-directed, with multiple opportunities for student leadership. After a few months of guided practice in academic and social skill development, students should be running the classroom more and more. By the end of the school year, our role should more resemble that of coach than of a teacher.

In short, the key ingredient for any successful educator is self-reflection. With the definition of success being growth in personal, cognitive, and skill development, successful teachers are able to develop connections. Nurturing authentic, maturing relationships lays the groundwork for twenty-first century schools to form the critical thinking, interdependent, world citizens we all need. The foresight outlined in this book develops the trains of thought for teachers to bring out the best in themselves and their communities

In the mindset of nurturing personal responsibility, the format of this book can be accessed in multiple ways depending upon the interest of the reader. Each chapter can be read independently based upon specific topic interests, or one can read the entire book cover to cover to experience a full year in the life of a teacher. Each chapter begins with a generic scenario, written in the second person.

You, the main character, then get to explore how to resolve some of the underlying issues teachers continually face.

Some terms that I use throughout the book may need some additional explanation:

- **Empathy Break:** This is my attempt to highlight the self-reflection process veteran teachers go through dozens of times each day. The more empathic we are, the better bonds we form, and the more each participant in the education process can thrive.
- **Backward Planning:** Breaking down instructional processes into a discrete step by step sequence to reach an end goal is vital to making the educational process clear and manageable. In my experience, backward planning is equal in importance to empathy breaks. This is akin to unpacking an idea. Both terms are intended to add clarity to the conscious planning that is required in successful content, skill, and social development.

It is in this spirit of collaboration and striving towards bringing out the best in each school relationship, and each school culture, that I invite you to expand your own Empathy Based Solutions.

1. Welcoming Students to a New School Year

YOU have not slept well over the past week. Some of your veteran colleagues have said they also get anxious before the first day of school. You try to remember how worried you were as a child the night before school, but it is mostly a blur. Right now, nervous anticipation doesn't come close to describing how you feel. It is midnight and you are still lying awake in bed. You go through your mental checklist of what you have prepared for tomorrow . . .

- ▸ Roster
- ▸ Student information sheets
- ▸ Class syllabus
- ▸ Seating chart

What are you missing? You think you have thought through everything, but doubt keeps you awake when you really want to rest.

The day starts normally—well, normally for a teacher. You are up at 6 a.m. and at school by 7:30. You look around your room. Is everything all set? Your problem is that you don't know what you want to do on this first day, and you are overwhelmed with options. You have choices to make, and the students are about stream in.

What is your next move? Here are the options or situations you may have to deal with. You:

1. Jump straight into content—p. 3
2. Offer fun and games—p. 5
3. Deal with a behavior problem—p. 5
4. Administer a test on Day One—p. 7
5. Play "get to know you" games—p. 7
6. Make students earn their way into your room—p. 9
7. Perform a writing assessment on the second day—p. 11
8. After losing all essential resources, you improvise—p. 12
9. Deal with a parent who wants to have a discussion with you—p. 13

Following is a discussion of each option. You can move from one to the next, or you can jump between options at any time.

Option 1. Jump Straight into Content

YOU decide that you will get to know your students through actual practice. Let them come in. You're ready. Anyway, according to the pacing guide, who has the time to get to know their students? You have too many content standards to cover. You have already done your backward planning for the year, and there isn't a day to waste. Let's jump straight into it.

The bell rings. Students have assembled in front of your classroom door. Immediately you see Maria playfully knock over one of her friends as all of the students jostle for position lining up. Do you say anything? *No.* Your choice is to jump into content, with no time to spare.

You step aside as the students enter quietly. Yes, you have a seating chart, so you have assigned seats, and you have a book waiting at each seat for each student. You know this is rare, but after pleading with the administration, asking your colleagues for extras, and searching in the forgotten corners of the school, you now have a full set of class books.

You stand in front of the room, and a quiet hush descends. This is your moment. This is the reason you have had trouble sleeping during the past week. You remember what your grandfather told you: "You can only meet someone once." What will be the first true words you say to the class to solidify your position of authority as a teacher? The wording comes to you almost as fast as you can wrap your mouth around it: "Open your books. We're ready to work."

Wow, that sounded great. Forward looking. High expectations. All business. The problem is that you might be ready to work, but the students aren't. They still have unresolved questions.

First, humans are social animals. As infants, we all quickly realize that there is more in the unknown world for us than in the known world. We need a social safety net, a net that includes each other, to figure out our world. The students in your class are not going to be able to work until they know all about the setting in which they will be working.

Second, humans are still animals. We need to be trained to do anything. Inherent in our training is repetition and high expectations for growth.

You quickly realize your mistake. You are facing students who are not trained and do not yet know the social environment in your classroom. Trouble is not far behind.

"What page should we be on again?" a voice blurts out from the back of the room.

"I don't have a book. Who stole my book? Excuse me, teacher, I need a book."

"Anybody have a pencil? I need a pencil. Anybody?"

A cacophony of voices pushes you back against the wall. What have you started? Within seconds, every child is talking, either to the next child or across the room.

The class period cannot go by fast enough for you as you scramble to pull them back to the lesson. During the rest of your time with this class, you find yourself explaining the instructions over and over again. It takes a considerable amount of energy to quell your ever-rising frustration.

The next day more than 90 percent of your students have attempted the assignment. They want to start off the year on a positive note and create a good first impression. Unfortunately, few have demonstrated competency—and it was a standard from the previous year. You remember talking with last year's teachers during staff orientation time, and you know these children received solid instruction. What was the problem?

A realization screams in your head—you must invest and focus on personal relationships. Children start off the school year with three essential questions:

- ► Who are you?
- ► Who are they?
- ► What do you really want from me? (In other words, how can I meet your expectations?)

The more quickly you answer these questions, the lower the emotional barriers—otherwise known as students' *affective filters*—will be for your students and the more prosperous everyone can be.

→ WHAT IS YOUR NEXT MOVE?—P. 3

Option 2. Offer Fun and Games

YOU have been so excited about starting your school year that you feel as though your skin is a paper-thin layer holding your being together. The problem is that your skin *is* paper-thin. You want your students to like your class, but secretly you want them to like you. You have decided to start your school year investing time in making them feel comfortable in your room.

You ask your students to come in and sit anywhere they want. Early in the day, a stunned silence meets this offer. By midday, you find it difficult to get their attention and you are already talking over them. You ignore this first clue of students dismissing your authority—talking over you—and stick with your plan.

"I call this game 'Crossing the Line,'" you announce. "If what I call out is true for you, please take one step forward." You have seen this game played countless times. The leader calls out some benign statements at the beginning of the game and then goes into more personal ones. A prime example is starting with, "I ate breakfast" and then moving up to "I have problems with my parents." Just like stand-up comedy, timing is everything.

During first period, no one moves.

In second period, no one can stop laughing. You immediately realize the truth behind the old poker line—If you look around the table and you don't know who the rube is, then you are the rube.

In third period, you get some positive reactions, but students offer mixed reactions during the rest of the day.

After lunch, you realize that you threw a party for which your students were not emotionally ready. *Guarded* is the only word that describes how they reacted throughout the day. They don't know you, and when they met you, you were wearing the joker's hat.

Teachers are in the business of selling the importance of school—investing in the future by building in social and academic skills now. To get there, you need to sell seriousness and personal relationships. To do well, students need a serious attitude toward their work; in short, they need to care. You may have made traction on personal relationships, but at what expense? Do they take your class seriously? Maybe. Maybe not. The problem is that you don't know.

Crossing the line—it's a terrific idea, but it is a little too soon. Balance is the key. Everything needs to be earned, including fun and games.

→ WHAT IS YOUR NEXT MOVE?—P. 3

Option 3. Deal with a Behavior Problem

WELCOMING your class, you decide to have them line up outside of your classroom. You saw another teacher do this and it looked impressive. That other teacher's students seemed attentive and even enthusiastic. You are skeptical about trying it yourself, because you know things are rarely what they seem from far away, but you decide to try it anyway. You ask students to line up before they enter your room. Your mistake is that you only got a snapshot of what your colleague was doing. Without knowing her full game plan, you find yourself taking a metaphorical exam after reading only half of the book.

You see the problem a mile away. The students who line up furthest from you started to smash into each other's shoulders. What starts off as benign jostling quickly intensifies into a simulation of alpha rams trying to shatter each others' skulls. In the ten seconds it takes you to recognize the problem and get there, two boys' backpacks are down and glares are on.

Voices ring throughout the hallway, "Fight. Fight. Fight. Fight...." Students circle around the two boys. You push your way through. Your voice and body thrust themselves into the ensuing chaos. "Stop it!" you scream.

"Make me," the larger boy responds, never taking his eyes off the one he's picked as an antagonist.

You stand there, aghast. Is this really the first impression your new students want to make?

You command both boys to come with you. Another teacher pops her head out of her class to see about the commotion. You ask her to watch your class as you escort the boys to the main office.

While you are filling out the discipline referrals at the main office, your brain screams out, "What happened?!," "What should I have done differently?"

That night, you replay this sequence through your head dozens, if not hundreds, of times. Proximity. You were too far away. Lining them up wasn't the problem. You suddenly remember the old adage, "Either you work the room or the room works you."

Empathy Break

What is the first day like, from the students' perspective? One way to describe it is that each is a gut-wrenching bundle of nerves. All children want to belong, but few know how.

Your solution comes into focus: Be social with your students. As they walk up, greet them. Shake each child's hand. As you stand in the hallway, talk with them. Be genuine with them as you make eye contact.

Soon, you find yourself saying such things as:

"Hey, nice new shoes."

"You excited about being back?"

"This is going to be a fun year."

"You put a lot of time in getting ready for school today—it shows."

"What is your schedule? Oh, I heard Ms. Patel is fantastic."

Soon, you are talking with random students you don't know who aren't even on your class roster. You can have a lot of mini-conversations during the three-minute passing period. Be mindful that children are always watching you. When you talk to them in the hallway, they see someone who is approachable, present, aware of their surroundings, and there.

Essentially, model the behavior you want students to exhibit on a daily basis. Keep your conversation light, school-focused, and optimistic. (It is the first day, after all). In the same way that nature abhors a vacuum, human beings abhor social groupings in which there is an absence of leadership. The importance of modeling what you want out of the people with whom you work cannot be understated.

➜ WHAT IS YOUR NEXT MOVE?—P. 3

Option 4. Administer a Test on Day One

LAYING down the law is your top priority. Students need to know you are the unquestionable authority in the room. As you were preparing for your year weeks ago, you came to the conclusion that giving a content-specific test was your ideal answer.

"Ladies and gentlemen, thank you for taking out your pens or pencils. You have the class period to finish this test. When you are done, please read quietly." That sounded great—just like you practiced it.

You stand at the front of the room and watch three things happen simultaneously. First, every child is taking you seriously—wow, that feels awkward and powerful. Second: Within the first ten minutes, students' real school personas come out in force. Some of them really go at the test. You can smell their dedication to success. But you quickly see that these students are the exception. Most students are going through the motions. Yes, they attempt the test, but they give quick, random answers and skim over the materials, so you can see that their enthusiasm for school has transformed into a "doing school" façade. Third, the overwhelming number of students leave your room with their shoulders slumped.

The year is a marathon. What did your students get from their time with you? Do you really want students to feel dejected right out of the gate?

You may argue, rightfully so, that you want your class to be challenged. From your experience, it is true that most students rise to the challenge. But the undeniable truth is that every construction project depends on the quality of the scaffolding, the construction materials, and the tools required to build. You teach to provide that list—scaffolding instruction to build up; academic resources; and the skill development to access those resources. Now go back to the initial question: Do you really want students to feel dejected right out of the gate?

Even your top students will often feel as though they are coming up short. That message is the opposite of the purpose and promise of school.

➜ WHAT IS YOUR NEXT MOVE?—P. 3

Option 5. Play "Get to Know You" Games

AFTER talking with your colleagues about their first-day preparations, you find that the majority of time spent on your campus for the first day will be teacher talk. Most teachers will present their syllabus and expectations for the year. Very logical. Very predictable. You want to make your own mark and big opening. You want to be unique and memorable. This isn't like the fun-and-games option. You are already aware of the limitations of being a friend to students. You don't want that label. The staff won't respect you, and the students will walk all over you.

"Welcome to my classroom," you say, because you want to be cordial and professional, not distant and cold-hearted, but you also don't want to give away your inherent position of power as the leader of the classroom.

Because of multiple class periods, you have another fresh beginning to make a first impression. You have already lined up students outside. This time, you stand closer to the group as a whole so you can reach any student within three strides. Students have already earned their way into your classroom. Most students have finished the first-day questionnaire, and you have already given an overview of the syllabus. You have twenty minutes left—what to do?

"Congratulations on demonstrating that I can trust you to work well and follow through on what I expect you to do," you tell them. You have always found it imperative to acknowledge positive behavior immediately. You try to make the first words that come out of your mouth ring positive and true as well as pick up where you left off before.

Matching students' optimal attention span, you limit yourself to ten minutes to present the key elements of your syllabus. Then you address the class:

"I just finished telling you about the syllabus for the year. Now I want to answer three questions I think you have about the coming school year. The first question I think you want answers to is 'Who are you?' As I talked about the syllabus, I spoke about me. I will continue to be as open as I possibly can to give you more information about who I am. I think your second question is 'What do you expect from me?' As you saw in my discussion of the syllabus, I never expect you to be perfect, but I do expect you to be aware of the needs of others so we can all thrive in this classroom.

"For the next fifteen minutes, I am going to try to help you answer what I think is your third question, 'Who are the other students in the room?' As part of helping you succeed, I will try to make you feel completely comfortable in this classroom, which is our 'learning world.' To accomplish that, you need to know the people you will be working with. So let's get started."

You have sewn the ground so the only things you need now are the seeds. You can now attempt pretty much any "get to know you" game that you have experienced before: people bingo, crossing the line, musical chairs—anything, because you have laid down a structured respectful foundation.

You can hear your mentor teacher's voice breaking down the year into four major parts. Right now you are in stage one—the honeymoon phase. Children will do their best to show you, "See, I'm a good kid." This first phase can last one day or two weeks, depending on multiple factors, but don't ever believe that phase two isn't coming. Regardless of how long you teach, or how well you know the community, you will find that students need the trial phase of "what can I get away with?" as part of their quest for independence. When you are a new teacher, this phase can last 2 weeks or this can last the entire year. It all depends on how you deal with it. By laying down your "I'm all business" persona with consistency, following through, and creating connections to home, you will get to know your "clients" and then enter the golden phase, stage three. In this phase, your students will take you seriously. They want to be there, and you just need to run a positive machine. This phase lasts until Memorial Day during a traditional calendar and two weeks before the end of the term for a year-round calendar. Stage four is inevitable. Students will always enter the "I'm done" phase in which they are thinking about summer. This is when you assign projects and group work.

It is essential to keep the following in mind: whatever behavior you put up with in the first week, you and the rest of the students will live a more extreme version of it throughout the rest of the school year. Do not tolerate any student or group of students commandeering your classroom.

Just to review: Students start off the school year with three questions: Who are you? What do you expect from me? and Who are the other students in the room?

You have already shown who you are: someone who commands respect, who expects students to work together in your room and who respects students enough to talk *with* them, and not *at* them, in the hallway.

The "What do you want from me?" question was answered with your actions and clear limit setting. You want students to be respectful and focused or else they wouldn't have earned the privilege of being in your room. The syllabus was a beautiful hands-on guide for the long-term vision encompassing your vision for the school year.

"Who are the other students in the room?" is the only question you have not answered fully. Never assume that students know everyone else in the room. The goal of school is equal parts academic and social growth. For anyone to mature on both fronts, they need to work in a safe predictable environment. The best way to have a predictable environment is to know those with whom you are working. Thankfully, you have already thought of some solutions.

Too often, students play the "Find Someone: Get to Know You Bingo Sheet." This is good but usually overdone. If you want to go with this, try to come up with novel entries encompassing all facets of being a kid: "Dreams of flying." "Argues with parents about doing chores." "Can speak two languages correctly and can pretend to speak a third." "Did nothing worthwhile over the summer." "Loves to build stuff." "Has a secret talent—ask me what it is." You are a creative adult. You can come up with more.

Only after you have set up the parameters of your classroom, does the exercise "Crossing the Line" (Option 2 in this chapter) make sense.

➜ WHAT IS YOUR NEXT MOVE?—P. 3

Option 6. Make Students Earn Their Way into Your Room

A PRIMARY role of teachers is to be contributing members of society. When you look at the rest of the staff, you notice that the most respected teachers are the most approachable, not only with students but with adults. Things seem to flow effortlessly for them. Why is that? You know from your own personal history that everyone struggles in life. Why do things seem to come so much easier for these teachers?

You decide to take the time and observe one of your colleagues. You ask them beforehand if you can swing by for ten minutes during your preparatory period on the first day of school to see how a veteran starts off the school year. Gracious and team-oriented as always, Ms. Cruz says, "Of course."

When the students and you arrive at the same time to Ms. Cruz's class, the first thing you notice is that her classroom door is closed and she is outside talking to any student who passes by. There seems to be a playful atmosphere encompassing her personal space. When the students flock around her, she motions them along. You see that the first day of school shouldn't bring fear; it should be embraced as an opportunity for a new start.

You hear your principal's voice from just a few days ago at the staff meeting saying that all children want to do well but not all of them know how. The school's mission is to empower them to thrive socially and academically while promoting independence and personal ownership of their lives.

Once all of the students have arrived, Ms. Cruz stands where she can see the entire class. Students are lined up shoulder to shoulder, facing Ms. Cruz. She chooses a central place to stand where she is three steps from each of her more than thirty students. She starts to talk as she paces from side to side. Anytime a student whispers to the next child or even takes his or her eyes off of Ms. Cruz, she looks at the student and waits for that student's attention. The second the student decides to refocus his or her attention back on Ms. Cruz, she immediately says, "Thank you. Now you are doing things right." Instead of belittling or talking down to students, she positively redirects them to the behavioral norms to be successful. This interaction could easily become a game in which students feign goofiness, but Ms. Cruz's seriousness and calm trumps juvenile distractions. Just maintaining a focused listening posture for multiple minutes is a skill that doesn't come naturally and needs to be taught. She is all business, but the delight of what she does shines through.

"Welcome to another great school year! How great it is to see you today. This school year is as terrific as you want to make it. My job is to help you put into practice successful habits so you can become the person you want to be."

Motioning to the doorframe, she continues in her modulated voice, "This door frame is your visual clue that you are now entering a learning world. You can play and be social with your friends out here in the hallway, but when you pass though this doorframe, I expect you to shift to our world of work.

"I'm going to take roll out here in the hallway. When I call your name, please step forward and I will give you your seat number and this questionnaire. If anyone talks during this time, we will start over. This is a team effort, and I know you can focus."

As she starts to call names, she greets each student individually, making eye contact while shaking hands. There is never any mystery of who is in charge. She is standing near the doorway so she can see into her classroom and down the line of students at the same time. As expected, two students who are furthest from her start to giggle in the back of the line. She walks the walk regarding consequences. Without raising her voice, she talks into her classroom, "We're going to need to start over. Two of your colleagues have decided to be off-task. Please line up outside again."

Remarkably, without complaint, students exit the class, and reestablish the shoulder-to-shoulder line. Ms. Cruz starts from the top of the roster again, shaking hands and making eye contact with each student as he or she enters the room. This redo runs much more quickly. The students who are still waiting in line out of their own anticipation of entering the room naturally stop distractions and focus. You glance at the time. Even with two "redos," this entire endeavor lasted only five minutes. The product is every student sitting in his or her assigned seat, on-task, filling in a questionnaire so Ms. Cruz can best personalize instruction.

It is clear that within a matter of five minutes Ms. Cruz has laid out her behavioral and academic expectations, as well as personal and group incentives for both. Students earned the privilege of being in her room. By calmly maintaining her focus on doable high expectations, she has established herself as the unquestioned authority in the room.

As you walk out the door to go back to your own classroom, you see Ms. Cruz still working the room. She has set up her classroom so she can effortlessly reach each student's desk within a matter of four strides. She whispers compliments that one would hear from a coach: "I like your clear hand-writing." "Don't forget to put your name there." "Wow, you are almost done." "Are you sure that is your best work so far?"

You decide that because it is easier to go from "No" to "Yes" than from "Yes" to "No," you will channel Ms. Cruz and students will earn everything in your room. Repetition is the key to understanding limit setting. You think, rightfully so, that the best way for students to take you and your classroom seriously is to have them follow the same routine of lining up outside for the first three days of school. Congratulations. Your school year is off to a terrific start.

But how do you spend your time with students once they are in your classroom?

➡ WHAT IS YOUR NEXT MOVE?—P. 3

Option 7. Perform a Writing Assessment on the Second Day

IT is hard to hit a balance between being stern and welcoming. You have thought about trying the stern approach, where you do all of the talking and tell students what to do. What you have yet to consider is the possibility of open-input critical thinking.

For you to build meaningful relationships and foster academic and social growth, you need to know your students. Because the act of writing employs so much critical thinking, it really provides a superior snapshot of how children think.

On the second day—the day after you laid out your social and academic expectations for students—you could use an in-class snapshot. After much introspection, you come to the conclusion that the writing prompt you offer should match your goals.

You stand in front of the seated class and welcome them to Day Two. In essence, you started to work your students before now, because you were in the hallway talking to them—asking them how they slept and how their first day was yesterday. In that way, you showed them that you care about the whole child. Now, the bell rings on the second day of school and your class continues where they started yesterday, lined up shoulder to shoulder, with all eyes on you. If the students' line represents one side of a triangle, you are standing at the apex, so you can reach any of your more than thirty students in a matter of three steps.

The moment the bell rings, you start talking, interjecting your voice in the three-second silence following the school bell. "Great job," you congratulate them. "You have demonstrated a beginning understanding of how I expect you to think beyond yourself and work as a team. When you enter the room, there will be a writing prompt waiting for you on your desk."

Children need positive strokes. You find that they are always initially amazed that you can be so prepared. You find that it is really simple to just ask the previous class to leave the class set of instructions centered on each desk before they leave. The more routines you overtly teach and delegate to students, the more time you get to spend one-on-one, getting to know your clientele.

Standing at your doorway, so you can see down the line of students and into your classroom, you shake each student's hand. This gives you a moment to do multiple things at once. By looking at students' averted eyes and slumped shoulders, you can easily identify which students had a rough morning and are distracted. As the weeks progress, you can pull aside these same students and talk with them, because your class can be trusted to follow through on your starting routine. Investing the time to talk with students and show them individual concern is a brilliant preemptive strike to eliminate classroom disruptions, which steal instructional minutes. This moment also gives you time to model appropriate handshake greetings and make appropriate physical contact with each of your students. You find that many students go through their entire day without physical contact, which is the direct opposite of our needs as physical beings.

It significantly raises your confidence to discover that you only have to start over and have students line up two more times until they are able to enter your "learning world" without talking. They are learning to take your consistency and high expectations seriously. You are confident that within four school days, students will be able to earn the privilege of entering your class without lining up first, because you have taught them what to do. Students can rise to the level of social interaction you expect.

➔ WHAT IS YOUR NEXT MOVE?—P. 3

Option 8. After Losing All Essential Resources, You Improvise

YOUR class is about to enter. You swear you put your stack of student questionnaires and syllabi right here. The only things you see clearly around you are numbered desks and chairs.

Breathe. Yes, you need these handouts for your first lesson. The last thing you want to project is disorganization. You take pride in being organized. Organization and congeniality are two requisite skills of being a teacher. Unfortunately, at this moment in time, you are not organized.

The bell rings; students are gathering outside your door.

Your humanity needs to shine through. Be professional and improvise. You realize that you don't really need any handouts to complete your lesson. What do your students really need on the first day? They need to feel confident that you care. They need to feel secure.

You step into the hallway with your classroom door open behind you. You stand where you can see all of your students and walk up to any one of them within three strides. You then greet them: "Welcome to a year in which all of you will grow and develop skills that will improve your lives."

Your mind is racing while you talk through your memorized script about your classroom being a learning world. You realize that even the best managers learn to fake leadership when they need to.

Your goal today is to focus on answering their three questions: Who are you? What do you expect from me? and Who are the other students in the room? You remember advice from one of the most brilliant teachers you have ever met: record a video of the students answering these questions. On the first day of school, students can brainstorm their answers. On the second day, you will make a video recording of your students answering these questions to the best of their ability. Because you only will show this video in your classroom, you won't need release forms. Other times for showing the video are the annual open house and the last day of school. Students will see how much they have grown and developed in just a few short months.

To pull this off, you will need to structure your expectations accordingly. Now that students have earned their way into your classroom, you will need to prepare them for the video exercise and alert them to your expectations for their behavior. You write the three questions on the board, saying, "Today, by the end of this class period, you will have prepared and practiced for tomorrow's video. Over the next twenty minutes, I expect you to get up and introduce yourself to at least ten other students in the room. Tomorrow I will be videotaping you saying your responses to these questions. I will show you this video on the last day of school so you can see how much you have grown and developed over time."

You call one of friendliest-looking students to the front of the room. Because students have earned the privilege of being in your room, and they want to make a good first impression, catcalling disruptions do not occur. You reach out your hand and introduce yourself to this student. Pointing to the front board for a prompt, you ask this student these three questions. She responds with a lot of "I don't know's."

You remind yourself to have patience—this is mild roadblock. She is obviously uncomfortable being singled out in front of the entire class. The truth of the matter is that they need time to practice, and are tired of watching.

Your exit instructions are vital: "This will get easier the more you practice. You have my permission to start with one or two of your friends, but within the next four minutes, I want you to try to talk to someone new. Let's go." And with the last command, students slowly get up and mill around your classroom. For many students this is new ground, because they spend so much of their day sitting and getting talked at. You need to model shaking hands with students and prodding some of them to be more involved.

The most important thing is that you put on your socializer hat and work the room. This gets easier as you do it more, in just the same way it will get easier for students to talk with each other the more they do it.

What appeared to be a lost day turns out to be a great day. After twenty minutes, ask students to return to their desks. This may take longer than you hoped, but they will learn this skill over time. If there is time left, students can practice what they plan on saying tomorrow. This is an ideal opportunity for your more social students to be themselves and not get blasted for it.

→ WHAT IS YOUR NEXT MOVE?—P. 3

Option 9. Deal With a Parent Who Wants to Have a Discussion with You

As you are trying to get your students organized to enter your classroom, a man whom you have never met approaches you in the hall. Who is this person? Is this a parent?

"Hi. Do you have a minute? I'd like to talk to you about my daughter, Caitlin," he says.

Your heart sinks. You have heard about helicopter parents, steamroller parents, and even mortar shell parents. Helicopter parents hover over their children or fly in and save their children and fly out. Steamroller parents roll over any problems facing their children, making the parent think that ignoring the problem represents actual parenting. Mortar shell parents are the worst of the bunch. They emotionally explode when you least expect it, knocking out anyone in their way. You don't know what type of parent is standing before you, but you know you don't have the time to find out right now.

"I'm sorry, I can't talk right now," you reply. "I need to get to my students. You can contact me later through the main office to schedule a time for a parent conference."

"This will only take a minute," he persists. "I'm really concerned about Caitlin's lack of progress last year, and I thought if I talked with you now we can make a plan together. It is important that you know that Caitlin is special. This is what I have in mind . . . "

You are only half listening. The moment for you to project your authority to your class and springboard your school year is quickly slipping away. Your students are starting to circle and talk in cliques. Some are not in the line but are instead venturing in and out of your classroom searching for you. You know you need to take control of the situation.

"Excuse me, sir," you interrupt him. The bell rings, and students don't know what you want them to do. Two boys start jostling each other in back of the line. The cacophony of noise coming from your students is getting louder, and here you are stuck with this seemingly self-centered parent. You feel like you are trapped in Edvard Munch's *The Scream*.

The parent continues to talk at you. "Excuse me, sir!," you say sternly. "I have a responsibility to my students right now. Please call or e-mail me later." You start to walk away.

"You don't have to be so rude to me!" he calls. "I'm trying to look out for my daughter, and you can't give me any time. I can see you don't care about my daughter's success, and I'm going to make sure other parents know it!" His voice gets louder with each syllable. His stance seems threatening, as well.

You have your class's attention now.

The first thing to keep in mind is to breathe. Being a teacher requires thick skin. You know he is just trying to provoke you. Yes, there will always be rumors about each and every public servant. You need to be your own moderator of truth. Breathe. People are watching you, and the most important of those are your students.

This is the perfect teachable moment. If you want your students to know when to walk away, you need to model that behavior. You turn your back again to address your class. Behind you, the parent throws up his arms in disgust, yelling, "I'm going to talk to the principal!"

There is a chorus of "Ohs" from the students who are the furthest from you. You turn your head and stare them down. Without saying a word, your problems vanish. The students in the back of the line become quiet and even take a step back. The parent, knowing his moment is gone, storms down the hallway toward the main office.

You know the principal. You know the front office staff. You have acted professionally. During the entire incident, your focus on your job, serving your students, never wavered. Now you are here with more than thirty students staring at you. They are lined up in the way you wanted, and you didn't even have to say a word to them.

You take a cleansing breath, in through your nose and out your mouth. You decide to put on your poker face and get started.

➜ WHAT IS YOUR NEXT MOVE?—P. 3

2. Lesson Planning and Teaching Strategies

YOU may be working at a school with a sequenced planning guide and the explicit directions to follow it, or you may be working with just a teacher's edition. Whatever materials you are using, you are still responsible for creating your own nuanced, moment-by-moment instruction.

As you sit down to plan your school year, you think about the scope of your job. With so many students, so many Individual Education Plans (IEPs), and so much content, how can you or anyone else hope to do it all?

To answer that question, you first need to map out your year against the content you are required to teach.

Planning Lessons for the Year

Pacing is the key to successful year-long teaching. Breaking the year into four-week units enables you to cover the teaching standards you are required to cover and circle back to reinforce the essential skills to understand these standards. Your first move is to look at the school calendar and allocate time so you are not in the middle of a unit during an extended school holiday. It takes true time management to end the year with all of your units completed on time. It is the rare year when this can happen. Closing off the unit with minimum compromise of your learning objectives is essential.

So now you have your year planned. But what happens if things don't go as you planned? What if you lose a half day of instruction to an assembly or sudden unannounced visitors or, worse, a natural disaster closes the school for several days? You should always leave room for a contingency plan; a few extra days of time somewhere in the schedule that gives you the opportunity to make up for lost instruction.

You can't plan for everything, though. What do you do when you run out of extra time to make up for an interruption? Your first reaction is to cut content, but you are afraid that shortening your unit lowers essential skill development time for students and eliminates key academic information they will need to build on later in the school year.

Instead of cutting content, you try changing the way you think about how you spend the time you have with the content. You remember that Bloom's Taxonomy of Learning Objectives (Bloom et al., 1956) outlines how assessment drives instruction. You decide to reassess the themes and skills you want your students to be fluent in. It seems that most of your students' work centers on lower-level thinking prompts that are focused on description. You believe you must make some changes so that you can direct students to think critically, which is more important than being able to regurgitate basic facts.

To get students started, you focus on what Bloom calls Knowledge and Comprehension, which is essentially retelling the content taught in class. For a little bit of lift, you expect students to take the content apart—Analysis—and use Application to put the content to use. Your end goal is the top of the ladder—Synthesis and Evaluation. Synthesis questions include:

- What would you predict/infer from. . . ?
- What ideas can you add to. . . ?
- How would you create/design a new. . . ?
- What might happen if you combined. . . ?

- ▸ What solutions would you suggest for. . . ?

Evaluation questions include:

- ▸ Do you agree. . . ?
- ▸ What do you think about. . . ?
- ▸ What is the most important. . . ?
- ▸ How would you place the following in order of priority. . . ?
- ▸ How would you decide about. . . ?
- ▸ What criteria would you use to assess. . . ?

Can a student take your instruction and bring together the essential concepts in a new way—Synthesis? Most of all, can you help students make informed decisions based on the content you are teaching—Evaluation? Essentially, the more you do this job, the more important you find it is to cut to the chase and move students to Synthesis and Evaluation as soon as you can.

Planning the Pace of an Individual Unit

You walk right by the same colleague's classroom and notice that a month has gone by and the posted teaching objective has not changed. You look through the window and notice he is sitting at his desk. You knock on the door, and he motions you into his classroom.

"Did you know that the Crusades spanned almost two hundred years?" he asks you. "I feel as if I have been teaching my unit on the Crusades for just as long. I just don't know how to move on and close it out."

You have already solved this problem for yourself, and you're ready to share your secret. "Have you ever heard of Madeline Hunter?" you ask. "She proposed an instructional model with seven essential components for an instructional model (Hunter 1994):

1. Review
2. Anticipatory Set
3. Objective
4. Input and Modeling
5. Checking Understanding
6. Guided Practice
7. Independent Practice

"The obvious goal is to foster independent practice. At the beginning of a unit, I focus on making explicit the objective and standards I will be covering. Often, this is a quick flip through the textbook, or a PowerPoint® of the main ideas I will be covering. My understanding is that Ms. Hunter would say this is the 'anticipatory set.' Everyone learns better when he or she has an idea of what is coming up. Then it is just a matter of breaking down the unit into four key areas and spending one week on each key area. I know that I often get tired of a unit after four weeks.

"I try to keep the underlying purpose behind my instruction consistent based on the day of the week. I try to not introduce new concepts on Mondays or Fridays. Mondays are usually devoted to reviewing instruction from the previous week. Tuesdays, I build on connections between last week's information and this week's new ideas. Wednesdays, I spend primarily on new material with a focus on guided practice. Thursdays I spend reviewing the new material and edge students toward more independent practice. And on Fridays I assess if students know the new material and can make connections to the previous week's work. Throughout all of this, students are working their way toward more and more independent practice.

"By structuring my class in this way, I find that students know what to anticipate," you finish up. "They see connections between one week and the next. Most of all, I take the seemingly huge unit and break it down to manageable bits."

Your colleague thanks you for your advice and agrees that he will pace his next unit differently.

Determining Learning Styles

Now that you have planned your year and your individual content units, you need to think about teaching strategies for communicating the content to your students. You think back to something your mentor teacher said to you: "Personal relationships enable access to content." What did she mean? After some thought, you realize that you need to know more about how your students take in content. How do they learn? Once you know that—once you have established a personal relationship with each student so that you know how each one learns—you'll be able to teach in a way that helps all of your students access your instruction.

According to psychologist Howard Gardner (1983), all people think and learn in different ways. His initial research focused on seven ways the brain may process the world:

Bodily-kinesthetic: Students who are primarily bodily-kinesthetic may seem jittery to the casual observer. They really do learn best by moving. Quite often, these are the students who get into the most trouble in school, because, according to adults, they "just can't sit still." Don't be afraid to get students out of their seats. Variations of musical chairs, hand-eye coordination activities, or any other incorporation of movement into your lesson will help make your content relevant to these learners.

Interpersonal: Locating interpersonal learners in the hallway is simple: Look at the center of a pack of friends, or whoever is talking the most and loudest, and there you will find America's future CEOs. Just like bodily-kinesthetic learners, interpersonal learners get into trouble for "acting out." (Often the bodily-kinesthetic learners are also interpersonal learners.) From the students' perspective, all they are doing is verbally processing, and then the conversation gets off-track. One student's innocent whispered question to another asking for clarification quickly devolves into a rehashing of last weekend's party. Successful teachers educate interpersonal learners to use their powers for good. Finding ways to bring them into the fold frees up what could be wasted time in redirecting and re-teaching them because you didn't see they weren't focused the first time. After every ten minutes of instruction, take thirty seconds and have students retell the content to check for comprehension with a partner. You can even have an interpersonal learner teach part of your lesson for the day.

Intrapersonal: These strong, silent types are America's future CFOs. Quite often, these students like their own space and need time to process new information. It may seem as though they are "spacing out," but more often than not they are just trying to incorporate the content you are presenting into their ever-evolving mental map of the world. An ideal way to get these students more involved in the class is to foreshadow your lesson for them while you are teaching. During one of your "think, pair, share" moments, when you cater to your interpersonal learners to talk about what is going on in class, you should be circling around the room monitoring student engagement. This is a perfect moment to whisper to one of your intrapersonal learners, "In 2 minutes, during the whole-class discussion, I will ask you this question." Tell the student a question pertinent to the lesson. "Do you know what you might answer?" This is a great way to weave the intrapersonal learner into the fabric of your ongoing class explorations.

Linguistic: Allow students to retell content in their own way. What would Shakespeare's writings look like as text messages? Can a student articulate a specific step-by-step narrative of a math problem?

Logical-Mathematical: Spotting these students is as easy as looking at their binders. The students who are organized and can find a specific handout in a nanosecond are your logical folk. While these learners flourish with structure, such as cause-and-effect flowcharts, shades of gray throw them for a loop. They thrive on challenges, so stretch them. Expect these learners to answer the same math problem in three different ways. Pushing them to see the gray, to help them make more logical connections in their world, helps reinforce their thinking.

Musical: You will be able to locate your musical learners by the bounce in their step, as well as the rhythmic drumming of their fingers. Even the subtlest changes in teaching style appeal to these learners. Developing a rhythm to your presentation voice brings in musical thinkers. Creating rhythmic mnemonic devices helps them memorize basic facts.

Spatial: Identifying these learners is easy: look at students' shoulders (up and back) and eyes (they are usually looking up and are watchful of the world around them). In ancient times, these are the people who saved the tribe from animal predators. Today, these are students who thrive on seeing subtleties in text and pictures. The more concrete examples and visuals you can bring in, the more you can bring in these students.

After Instruction: Checking in with Students

The options in this chapter give you teaching strategies that help you connect content to all of the different learning styles in your classroom. After using any of the options, it is a good idea to "check in" with students to determine their level of understanding of content concepts. One way to do this involves hand signals. Start by saying the following:

"If you understand what was just presented—to the level that you can teach it to others—hold up five fingers on one hand. If you know it and just need a little practice, hold up three fingers, and if you are completely confused, hold up one finger. Honesty is critical. I will never allow one student to make fun of another student in my classroom. In addition, I will never yell at you for being honest and saying you need more practice to understand the lesson. So please be honest so I can best help you."

Obviously, students need a safe environment where they feel they can be honest with you. The most effective way to create a safe classroom is by investing in a personal relationship with each student. Another way is to make it clear that you will not tolerate any name-calling or bullying behavior in your classroom. In addition, you need to model the behavior you want from students; kindness must rule the day. Finally, always spin the positive. For example, instead of admonishing a linguistic student for talking out, say simply, "You have two ears and one mouth. Your ears outnumber your mouth. Use your ears first."

Now that you have determined the learning styles present in your classroom and have created a safe environment for learning, how can you diversify your lesson design so that *all* students can access the content? Naturally, your units should address as many learning modalities as possible.

Following are suggestions for teaching strategies that address multiple learning styles. These strategies were influenced by:

- ► Cathryn Berger Kaye, M.A.
- ► Ron Klemp, Northridge Middle School
- ► Bert Bower, Teachers Curriculum Institute
- ► Fred Jones, Fred Jones and Associates
- ► Jack Weinstein, Facing History and Ourselves

As you work through the strategies, remember that, ideally, the content shapes the lesson format. For example, if you are teaching about the American colonies in a social studies class, your lesson could include a colonial job fair, which would address multiple learning modalities: bodily-kinesthetic, interpersonal, intrapersonal, logical-mathematical, linguistic, and spatial. But what if you are teaching math?

In addition, throughout your use of the options, keep the classroom tone positive and stay away from sarcastic humor. Chances are you will have a handful of students in each class who either refuse to or who are reluctant to be involved. Instead of seeing them as outliers, or obstacles, turn their obstinate attitudes to your advantage.

Which teaching strategy will you choose for your new classroom first? You:

1. Create learning communities: Quote Exchange—p. 19
2. Have students teach students: Inside/Outside Circle—p. 20
3. Help students develop passionate opinions: Take a Stand—p. 22
4. Encourage students to develop empathy: Structured Argument—p. 23
5. Hold chart-paper reflection time—p. 25
6. Create your own content-specific interactive presentation structure—p. 26

Following is a discussion of each option. You can move from one to the next, or you can jump between options at any time.

Option 1. Create Learning Communities: Quote Exchange

THIS activity is an ideal way to get students out of their seats and talking with each other. The ideal times to use this activity are the first week of a new class or after long breaks. It can also be used to preview or review a unit, or as a way to foster new learning pairs. Best of all, it is quick, no more than seven minutes of class time. Following are the multiple learning modalities accessed using this teaching format:

- Interpersonal
- Intrapersonal
- Linguistic
- Logical-Mathematical
- Spatial

Before starting, you gather a number of famous quotations related to the unit you are teaching. You find quotes on the Internet or in any number of published compilations. If you are starting off a unit on pre-reading skills with early elementary children, you can use pictures instead of quotes. For math, you can compile quotes regarding the values of determination, practice, focus, and diligence. The quotations shed light on the underlying purposes and values that you want students to glean from the content. You can use the same class set year after year.

Next, you cut strips of paper, one for each student and five extras. You write one quote on each, keeping the five additional quote strips as backup. Then you write the instructions for the activity on your board so that you don't have to repeat them over and over to students:

> Today's goal is for you to get to know multiple perspectives from other students about our upcoming unit of study.
>
> Step 1: Please read your quote.
>
> Step 2: Please think of why this quote is important to what we are studying.

Step 3: Please walk up to another person in the class, read your quote out loud, and then listen to their quote. If you like each other's quotes, trade.

Step 4: Please exchange quotes with at least five other people during the next five minutes.

You stand at the classroom door and hand each student one of the strips of paper. You tell students to read the instructions on the board. This makes them less reliant on you for every bit of direction. Then you start the activity.

Tips for Implementing the Activity

What is most important is that you are an equal participant in this activity. You will show students your engagement and approachability. You know that you can also redirect off-task students by joining the class.

"May I see your quote?" you ask the reluctant student standing next to you. He slides the scrap of crumpled paper in your direction. Your knowledge of your students at this moment is the critical factor in your next move. If the student is acting aloof for attention, limit-setting is appropriate. Chances are the student is being an obstructionist for reasons that have nothing to do with your classroom. Patience, encouragement, and steadfastness are your best reactions. Some sample conversation starters with this student may include:

"I know you are capable of being social right now."

"Who are you going to talk with first?"

"Let's practice what you plan on saying about your quote."

This student then says something like, "This activity is stupid." Don't take the bait. You don't have to justify your lessons to a child. You simply redirect him to refocus on the lesson.

→ WHICH STRATEGY WILL YOU TRY NEXT?—P. 19

Option 2. Have Students Teach Students: Inside/Outside Circle

THIS activity is an ideal way for students to work with everyone else in the classroom and review any material in less than ten minutes. While this lesson is more conducive to either preview or review of basic information, if you give students more time, you can also use it with higher-level thinking questions as well. This strategy can be used with any skill level or content.

For students who have completed an assignment, this method is a brilliant review and content reinforcer. For students who are half done, this lesson is a quick way to get them up to speed. Finally, for struggling students, this lesson brings to the surface the information they already knew coming into class and makes it pertinent to your class. Also, this lesson enables all students to practice speaking up for themselves and encourages student collaboration and engagement. Following are the multiple learning modalities accessed using this teaching format:

- ▸ Bodily-kinesthetic
- ▸ Interpersonal
- ▸ Intrapersonal

▶ Linguistic

A vocabulary review sheet is a perfect way to try this strategy with students. You start by describing your behavioral expectations in an encouraging, limit-setting way. Then tell students that you need them to get their vocabulary worksheets, a binder to write on, and a pen or pencil.

You ask your students to take out their vocabulary work. As you walk around the room, you ask them to write either a 1 or a 2 on the top of the vocabulary sheets. After you circle the room, you return to your "teaching spot" where all students can focus their eyes on you. You decide to wait fifteen seconds for their attention, because you have already learned that a teacher should never talk over students.

When it is quiet, you say, "You each have a 1 or a 2 written at the top of your sheet of paper. I would like all of the 1s to form a circle with your shoulders side by side. Those of you with 2s will also form a shoulder-to-shoulder circle. Please form your circle around the 1's group." Students form two "wheels," one inside the other. You then direct them to pair up, so that every Student 1 will be conversing with a Student 2.

Now you get your class's attention by whispering, "If you can hear my voice, please clap once." When all students are quiet, you continue explaining the activity to them: "The goal of this activity is for you to realize you know more than you think you do and for you to learn new content. I expect you to share your ideas, listen to other students, and take notes. You will have twenty seconds with your partner before you rotate to a new partner. Please shake hands with your current partner and say, "What do you know?"

For twenty seconds, the first pairs share what they know about what you are covering in class, and they fill in their vocabulary sheets. After twenty seconds, you tell students to rotate one person to their left. Every twenty seconds, you ask students to rotate. By continuing this rotation process, students work with a number of other students, reinforce their content knowledge, and learn from others.

Tips for Implementing the Activity

The first time you do this activity, allocate an extra three to five minutes to set up students in their circles. After the first time, students will understand how to line up and they'll be able to do it without help.

You can do this activity in your classroom with the desks moved out of the way, or you can also use an open area outside of your classroom. As any noise will be disruptive to other classes, alert colleagues when you will be doing this activity outside.

Use positive comments to model the positive interactions you want students to exemplify every day in your class.

The ideal place for you to stand is in the center of the two circles. You can then direct traffic. Once the circles are formed, do another loop and pair students. Have pairs shake hands. This simple gesture not only introduces working pairs but also helps you keep track of who is working with whom. Ideally, if you have an equal number of students, you are set. If you have an odd number of students, you will need to do double duty as leader and participant.

Throughout this mini-lesson, it is most important to stay consistent and manage time to ensure everyone interacts with each other.

→ WHICH STRATEGY WILL YOU TRY NEXT?—P. 19

Option 3. Develop Opinions: Take a Stand

Do you want students to develop passionate, respectful, insightful, critical voices and stand up for themselves? Then this is the lesson for you. You want students to think critically about the academic content they are learning and demonstrate mastery using their own authentic student voices. Following are the multiple learning modalities accessed using this teaching format:

- ▸ Bodily-kinesthetic
- ▸ Interpersonal
- ▸ Intrapersonal
- ▸ Linguistic
- ▸ Logical-Mathematical
- ▸ Musical

This activity can take anywhere from ten to thirty minutes and can be used for any content that could have two or more options (multiple ways to figure out a math problem—which one is best; two or more viewpoints on a historical event; interpretations of a story; multiple analyses of art; best ways to write a sentence; relevance of a primary source; breaking apart the scientific method; and so on).

To be successful, you want students to demonstrate an understanding of conflicting perspectives. To begin, you announce an issue. You then direct students to think about their stand on that issue. Their stand determines where they will now move in the room.

On one end of your classroom will be students who are pro—one side of a designated argument. On the opposite side of the classroom will be students who espouse the alternative perspective. You also designate a spot for undecided students.

Note: The following example centers on Kino from John Steinbeck's *The Pearl*. Use this example as a model for this activity.

You stand in front of your class to introduce this activity: "My goal for you this year is that you learn how to evaluate and apply what we do here in this class. Today, you will be standing up for your beliefs, literally. I will ask you to choose where you stand in the room based on your beliefs about Kino. If you think Kino is a cold-blooded killer, please stand on this side of the room." (You wave both hands to one end of the classroom, as a flight attendant would do to point to an airplane exit).

"If you think Kino is acting out based on being a victim of a racially divided community, please stand on this side of the room." (You wave both hands at the other end of the room).

"If you are undecided, please stand in the middle here. I recommend that you bring with you any of your class materials to support your arguments. Try not to simply stand with your friends. Make up your own mind."

You allow twenty or thirty seconds for students to choose where to stand. After they are all settled in place, you reinforce the goal of the lesson by saying, "Now it is time for members of each group to present the group's viewpoint to the other groups. In the ideal world we will alternate between both sides. So after your side makes a point, please wait for a response from the other side before you speak again. As you speak, remember that your goal is to persuade as many students as you can to move to your side of the classroom. Please keep your arguments to the topic, and keep in mind that personal attacks are always unwelcome in my safe classroom.

"When it is your turn to listen, if you hear an argument that changes your point of view, feel free to change groups. Who wants to start?"

You find that you have a number of volunteers—your interpersonal and logical learners—ready to make their cases to the other groups. Five minutes into this activity, you decide to ask the middle group, "What are some questions you would like answered that might help you choose one side or the other?"

Throughout the lesson, as you see student migrate from one group to the next, you interrupt the discussion and call to that student, "Wow! I didn't expect you to change groups. Which point swayed you to change your opinion?" As students reveal their thoughts and understanding of the content, you find that you are amazed at how much your students know and can think on their feet.

Tips for Implementing the Activity

Your three groups will vary in size. If you find that you have no students or a single student advocating for a side of the issue, you should stand with that student and advocate for that point of view. The teacher should moderate, in terms of who starts and how many are allowed within a group talk. Before you start, make sure to address your expectations from students during the course of the assignment.

Don't lose sight that the goal is to develop multiple points of view, not to reinforce current beliefs. Make it clear you just want to equalize the sides and that the arguments you will present do not necessarily match your personal beliefs. To solidify this point, you may want to move between groups multiple times throughout the lesson.

Your primary job throughout this lesson is equalization and inclusion. To keep a student from monopolizing the conversation, feel free to tell him or her, "You are allowed to share twice more today. Are you sure you want to use one of those times now?" In addition, try to get students from the two sides to alternate during the discussion by saying, "Good point. What does this side think of that point?" Overall, as the teacher, you will need to think on your feet and keep the conversation focused on the content.

You say, "In an ideal world we will alternate between both sides. So after your side makes a point, please wait for a response from the other side before you speak again."

➔ WHICH STRATEGY WILL YOU TRY NEXT?—P. 19

Option 4. Encourage Students to Develop Empathy: Structured Argument

AN ideal follow-up to "Take a Stand," this "Structured Argument" activity allows students to articulate their knowledge and evaluation of content in the setting of respectful debate. Following are the multiple learning modalities accessed using this teaching format:

- ► Interpersonal
- ► Intrapersonal
- ► Linguistic
- ► Logical-Mathematical
- ► Musical
- ► Spatial

As in the previous activity, "Structured Argument" can take anywhere from ten to thirty minutes and can be used for any content that could have two or more options. The features of this lesson structure are time flexibility, reinforcement of listening skills, and content reinforcement.

Note: The following example centers on a live example. Use this example as a model for this activity.

Before starting the activity, you draw a T-chart on the board. On the left side of the heading, you write "Reasons for limits on free speech." On the right side, you write "Reasons we should limit free speech." You then hold a whole-class discussion asking students to volunteer five supporting reasons for each of the two points of view in the T-chart.

You have students create reference notes from the T-chart on the board. You then tell them, "Today, we are going to participate in a type of debate called a 'structured argument.' During this structured argument, you should refer to your notes as a reference as you respond to each other."

You circulate around the room to clarify and guide students' work on their notes. At the same time, you write a 1 or 2 on each student's paper. You then tell students to pair up. Each 1 must find a 2 to partner with.

Each arguing pair will have a "1" and a "2." If you have an odd number of kids, assign one of the more confident students to take on two challengers for a total group of three students.

After your loop, you then return to your teaching position—the place in the class where you stand when you want students' attention. You say, "Let's get started. You should have in front of you, a completed (—or nearly completed—) "T-chart" listing five reasons on each side of the chart. Please turn your body to face your partner. To help you keep down the noise level in this class down to a workable level, I will flash the lights on and off to get your attention." You then model this jarring, strobe-like effect. "When you see the lights flash, I expect you to make sure you are listening to your partner. You will respond using the arguments in front of you. Try to stay focused on the issues."

You then give pairs the go-ahead: "Number 1s, please repeat after me." You start the conversation by highlighting one of the five arguments in the left column of the chart.

After the number 1s repeat what you say, you move on to 2s: "Now number 2s, how would you respond?" To keep students engaged, circulate around the class as the pairs argue back and forth. After about a minute, you flip the lights on and off.

You want to be positive when you talk with your class. "Great job being on task! Now number 2s, please repeat after me." You now highlight the arguments in the chart's right-hand column, and then you ask the 1s to respond.

Continue this process for a few iterations. The ideal part of this lesson structure is the time flexibility, social skill reinforcement of listening, content reinforcement, and fun. Ideally, eventually, one of your students starts off the choral response for the next round of the argument. You continue until the class has used all of the items on the chart.

Tips for Implementing the Activity

If you have an odd number of students, form a trio by assigning one of the more outspoken, confident students to take on two challengers.

Because you want students to practice independently, you can ask them to write out the script continuing the debate. The product can range from pictures to full-on courtroom-like transcripts, depending on your students' ability levels. This novel homework enables all students to demonstrate mastery of multiple points of view.

➜ WHICH STRATEGY WILL YOU TRY NEXT?—P. 19

Option 5. Hold Chart-Paper Reflection Time

IN this activity, students blog about content on chart-paper you provide, which is an ideal way for students to reflect on that content. In addition, students are exposed to their peers' perspectives. This lesson simultaneously promotes dialogue and checks for understanding. The added bonus is that the chart-paper products that are created can be used as reference guides throughout a unit or for end-of-year reflections. Following are the multiple learning modalities accessed using this teaching format:

- ▶ Interpersonal
- ▶ Intrapersonal
- ▶ Linguistic
- ▶ Logical-Mathematical
- ▶ Spatial

This activity can be used to review or preview what you are teaching, regardless of content. (For example, if you are teaching math, you can write multi-stage problems and students can write a narrative of how they figure out the problem—or pictograms based for early elementary.) The entire mini-lesson should take no longer than fifteen minutes.

You begin by preparing one piece of paper for every four students in your classroom. You know that larger sheets allow more students to write at once. At the center of the paper, you write one of the central ideas you have covered or will be covering in your classroom.

You break the lesson into three different stages:

Stage 1: Students walk around the classroom and respond to the prompt on the chart paper. The quieter students are for this step the better, as your focus is self-reflection. You urge students to write only their own ideas and initial their comments (five minutes).

Stage 2: On the second pass, students write responses to their peers' initial prompts. The paper has the look of an illuminated manuscript radiating out from the initial query in the middle of the page. You remind students not to talk so that they can focus on their writing (five minutes).

Stage 3: You have students team up with a friend and move about the room, discussing their own and other students' responses to the prompt. The more you are involved in these rolling conversations, the more insights you will gain about how students really think and the more students will take the task seriously.

After students leave, you read what the students wrote. You immediately gain new insights about what students are getting out of your class.

Tips for Implementing the Activity

Previewing the lesson expectations is essential for you to be successful implementing this activity. Make sure to balance time between quiet reflection and social engagement. Giving structured time for students to partner up also helps with mainstreaming students with special needs.

→ WHICH STRATEGY WILL YOU TRY NEXT?—P. 19

Option 6. Create Your Own Content-Specific Interactive Presentation Structure

Within a few months as a teacher, you have come to realize that self-reflection, empathy, and focusing on global concepts are the keys to planning multi-modal, interactive lessons.

First, after some self-reflection, you confirm what you already know about which styles are your strengths and which are your weaknesses. While it would be easy to teach to and reinforce your own strengths, your challenge is to create teaching structures for the areas in which you are weakest.

Second, as you have worked with your students, you have developed empathy for each and every one. You know more about how they learn now, and you want them to be successful in your classroom.

Third, to make your class most dynamic, you decide to create a history lesson plan that focuses on global concepts. Your state's specific standards and the Common Core State Standards pare down the dozens of individual skill-based norms into a manageable handful of concepts teachers are expected to circle back on and reinforce throughout the year. Students learn best when they can predict where your instruction is going and how it relates to relevant previous information they have already been exposed to.

To build your lesson, you must take the specified standards and what you know about your students and connect the two in a way that students can access the content. Because we build on prior knowledge, the more obvious you make the connections, the better your students will thrive. For your history lesson, in an attempt to make connections clear to students, you post a list of historical themes in your classroom:

- ▶ Quest for political power
- ▶ Influence of family/clan pressure
- ▶ Trade and economics (How to make money)
- ▶ Development of art to create a cultural identity
- ▶ Religious inclusion
- ▶ Religious intolerance
- ▶ Quest for equality
- ▶ Dishonesty
- ▶ Environmental backlash
- ▶ Environmental protection
- ▶ Doing the right thing
- ▶ Migration
- ▶ Inventions
- ▶ Celebrations

➜ WHICH STRATEGY WILL YOU TRY NEXT?—P. 19

3. Staff Meetings

As you head into your first staff meeting, you are filled with curiosity and caution. This is not like student teaching. This is the real deal. You are a full-fledged member of the staff. Your first priority is to put away your phone. Your second big priority is to bring in your planner to stay on top of everything.

You pause at the door to scout out the scene. The staff members who are there in body only line up as far away from the presenter as possible. There are cliques of teacher friends. Where people sit tells you a lot about the internal politics of your school.

You focus your energy on getting the lay of the land. It is easy to spot the primary movers and shakers on your staff—the loud ones. Keep in mind that the truths for your classroom are also in effect for the staff room. The true power in your staff lies with the connectors, those who help bring the staff together for common purposes and create a compassionate safety zone for the more recalcitrant staff members to speak out. (Malcolm Gladwell's book *The Tipping Point* [2000] highlights the value of the connectors). To make yourself invaluable as a staff member, you decide to be a connector, one of the voices for inclusion, and model involvement and commitment.

You look to the corners of the staff meeting. Your connectors are on the sides so they can watch the entire group. The people sitting close to the front are the go-getters. The people in the back want to be the first ones to leave. The teachers who feel the most disconnected with the rest of the staff are the ones who are grading papers or reading the news.

The more you think about it, the staff meeting is a mirror of your own classroom. How well are you integrating your students? Are you challenging them to mix it up socially? What are the dangers of staying in your comfort zone? How often would you expect your students or your colleagues to venture into new social territory? Your mind races with questions as you look for a place to sit.

What is your next move and how can you ready yourself for anything in a staff meeting? You:

1. Aren't sure you want to be a connector—p. 28
2. Arrive late to the meeting—p. 29
3. Prepare your room for a staff meeting—p. 30
4. Head a committee and present at a staff meeting—p. 31
5. Offer a suggestion at a meeting—p. 32

Following is a discussion of each option. You can move from one to the next, or you can jump between options at any time.

Option 1. You Aren't Sure You Want to Be a Connector

The politics that engulf any staff are hard to avoid. You think that the wisest political move is to decide that, during staff meetings, you will quietly observe. You wonder why your school has meetings at all, with e-mail, instant messaging, paper notes, and daily announcements available. Most information about school events, discipline strategies, and the school "vision" can be sent through e-mail.

In an effort to make sense of the unique social situation that is a staff meeting, you think back to your social studies instruction. Just today, your class discussion centered on the development of pre-hominids. For many millennia before formal language took root, humans made only grunting sounds. Nonverbal communication is still the primary communication tool among today's human beings. Anyone who travels for business can testify to the value of reading a customer's face, which cannot be done through teleconferencing. Applying this information, you decide to focus on eye contact, shoulders, and the gait of your colleagues as much as on the information being conveyed.

So, as you observe, you find you have another question: Why are most staff meetings structured so statically, with a presenter and the staff sitting as audience? You are lucky that your school's staff meetings are more interactive, flowing from small-group conversations to large-group discussions. Often, the staff is up and moves around the room.

You want to be taken seriously by other staff members, so you take these moments seriously. Should you sit toward the front of the room? Teachers who have been around for a while or have small children at home are fried at the end of the day, when staff meetings usually happen. They regularly sit on the sides or in the back of the room. Ideally, you will not choose to be one of those jaded teachers who bring work to a staff meeting. The direct message this sends is distance and disaffectedness. You consciously choose to avoid being described by either adjective.

Regardless of where you sit, compassion for your colleagues should rule your days. As you would set up your expectations for students in your classroom, you decide to have the same expectations for your colleagues. These are the people you will count on during unexpected times. Even the disaffected teachers warrant your time, because the fundamental truth is you never fully know someone else's story. A connector brings in diverse people. A connector tries not to judge.

Ultimately, you decide to sit next to a colleague you want to get to know better. Shared experiences are the foundation for blossoming friendships. As you sit down, you remember that everyone is there for the betterment of children. You know that it is up to you to find common interests with even the most unlikely staff member.

➜ WHAT WILL YOU DO NEXT?—P. 27

Option 2. You Arrive Late

YOU arrive late for a staff meeting.

"We decided to start without you," your principal snarls without even making eye contact.

You stand in the back of the room with your arms crossed tightly. Your heart races. "Is this the end?" you think. "Does my principal even know or care why I'm late?"

Empathy Break

What is it like to be a principal? As a new teacher, you really have more in common with your principal than you realize. Fundamentally, just like you, a good principal cares about students first and foremost; wants to keep his or her job; and needs to be able to roll with every day's unpredictable events. And, like your job as a new teacher, a principal's job isn't tenured. The tug-of-war of the principal's existence—between laying low and not making waves vs. pushing for greatness on the other, all the while not compromising standards—can easily pull apart a principal.

You stop thinking about your lateness for a moment, and you begin thinking about your principal's role in the school. To meet her main directive—uncompromising diligence to provide the best education for all students—she needs to be a staff unifier to be successful. As in any classroom, for all students to thrive, they need a safe, secure, compassionate, rigorous, and somewhat predictable environment filled with high standards. Your principal must work to achieve all of that for the entire staff. Although some principals are present in body only, you know that your principal exerts a great amount of effort to create that environment in your school.

So, with all of that on her plate, she has quite a bit on her mind. She needs cooperation from staff members to accomplish what she needs to do. And she doesn't know you well yet. What does your lateness mean to her? Are you aloof? Do you not take the meetings seriously? The last label you ever want is "not a team player."

Before you say something you may regret, you decide to be silent. The less you talk, the more power you have. You decide to be a contributor—albeit a quiet one—during the staff meeting. The more you think about your principal's point of view, becoming more empathetic toward him or her, the more your shoulders relax. You resolve to be on time for future meetings.

➜ WHAT WILL YOU DO NEXT?—P. 27

Option 3. Prepare Your Room for a Staff Meeting

You have just been told that the next staff meeting will be held in your classroom. The opportunity to host the meeting is your first opportunity to make yourself invaluable to the rest of the staff. As a connector, you want others to feel emotionally safe around you. How does your classroom display your values? Why was your classroom chosen? How can you use this moment to create bridges between you and other staff members?

After taking a deep breath, you make a To Do list to prepare for the meeting:

1. Take the time to read the agenda, which is usually sent out twenty-four hours before the meeting.

2. Breathe.

3. Look around your room. Don't just do a once-over—really look at your room. Look at it as an outside observer would.

4. Rearrange whatever you need to make your classroom inviting. Ask yourself: What things do I need to hide to give the impression I am organized?

5. Breathe.

6. Look at the clock and decide time allocation.

For this last item, you realize you should spend only thirty minutes getting your classroom together. Appropriately, the focus of the staff meeting is the staff meeting. You are just hosting the party.

With this list in hand, you wisely decide to highlight your organizational skills. You focus on putting away papers in an organized fashion. Being organized can never be underrated.

As you close your classroom door behind you, you remember a quote by John Wooden, a legendary UCLA basketball coach: "Be more concerned with your character than your reputation, because your character is what you really are, while your reputation is merely what others think you are." You know you can't control what others think of you. However, the better you feel about you—and there is a lot to feel good about—the more positive your character will be. With your positive character, your glowing reputation is soon to follow.

→ WHAT WILL YOU DO NEXT?—P. 27

Option 4. Head a Committee and Present at a Staff Meeting

YOU unexpectedly get called to the principal's office. It is early in March, so your first thought—and immediate worry—is that you are about to get pink slipped. The Ides of March are pink-slip time in most school districts.

You knock on your principal's door. "Come in. Do you have a minute? We need to talk."

You close the door behind you as he begins: "For a first-year teacher, you have made magnificent progress. I think it is time for you to take on some new leadership opportunities."

Your immediate reaction is relief that you are not being let go. Your next reaction is a question: "What is this 'opportunity,' and which veteran teacher passed it up so that you had to come to me?" You decide to listen. The more you hear, the more you realize that all leadership opportunities say more about you than about the job. You are seen as someone who doesn't drop the ball. With students, parents, and fellow staff members, you have been successful in presenting yourself as someone who can be held accountable. Don't take this lightly. These milestones, even if they seem like insignificant pebbles, are important.

Before you make a commitment, you ask for time to think about it overnight. No decision needs to be made in a rushed fashion. If your principal wants you to do something, he can wait twenty-four hours for your response. And if the answer needs to be delivered immediately, be assured that the opportunity is radioactive; walk away. A polite and gracious "Thank you, I'll think it over" gives you time and social points.

Take a pause and examine your life before you make new commitments. These questions need to be answered before you embrace a "yes:"

1. How does this new opportunity affect your ongoing quest for balance in your life? If you are working too hard, something in your life will snap. Just like with your physiology, homeostasis is king.

2. Keep in mind that something will go wrong with this new opportunity in one way or another. Will you have the additional time to put the project back on track after the derailment?

3. How will this new project affect your classroom life? You were hired to teach. Never put anything in front of your primary mission as an educator. This being said, growing your leadership skill set often reinforces and refines your classroom skill set.

4. How will this new role affect your growing workplace reputation? Will your coworkers see you as a leader as you take on this new opportunity?

5. How can you be inclusive? Can you build bridges with your colleagues? How can your rising ship elevate the tide for others?

As you are thinking about your new challenge, you come across an article about Fred Smith. His strategy to make Fed Ex go from good to great was to develop a company-wide conversation about "discretionary effort." What makes any organization thrive—especially schools—is how the employees dedicate themselves beyond the official work hours. Obviously, everything is a balance. Everyone is more productive if they are cognizant of balance. You can't and shouldn't work all of the time. Even marathons have finish lines. Simultaneously, how can you provide outstanding service? Will this extra commitment pay off by serving students better?

As part of this, you consider your own priorities. You want to be a team player and leader. You want to make yourself indispensable. And you want to do whatever you need to do to survive the next round of cuts—and there will be cuts. Everything you can do to create your own place on the staff will help you survive those cuts. Be prepared for a downside—the possible alienation of your peers. Regardless of your best intent, professional jealously and misunderstandings will happen. The best way around this is to do three things: (1) Enjoy life, and don't mire yourself in politics, (2) Take every opportunity to praise a colleague, and (3) Stay positive.

During your career, you will find that there are three types of people—doers, complainers, and watchers. No matter how pure your initial intent is, you may end up wearing all three hats. Overall, who do you want to be? That is the question you need to answer before you accept any new challenge.

➜ WHAT WILL YOU DO NEXT?—P. 27

Option 5. Offer a Suggestion at a Meeting

AS staff members discuss, yet again, an issue about which you feel passionate, you try to stay quiet, but your head is bursting. Don't these people realize the answer is right in front of them? As you reviewed the meeting agenda, earlier in the day, you saw that the issue was going to be up for discussion. You have been thinking about a solution for a while, and you want to talk about it at the meeting. You know that your solution is tied to a little more work for the rest of the staff, but you think that it's such a *great* idea that people will get on board immediately. However, you did not run it by any other staff member before presenting it here at the meeting.

The veteran teachers immediately hit you with intense stares. The ensuing quiet in the room lasts only seconds, but it feels like hours before someone else speaks.

You now have two choices—push your issue on, or give up the ship. If you decide to push, who will back you? You know that you need peer and administrative support to make meaningful change. You've heard about newbie teachers unintentionally burning bridges by coming on too strong. Giving up the ship may be a better option right now.

What you need is social capital with the staff. You're new, so you don't think you have much of that now. How do you bulk up your social capital account?

You can build your account in many ways. First, you need to show other staff members that you are responsible and accountable. At some point, the principal or a colleague will ask you for help, and you need to make yourself available to give that help. Another capital builder is kindness. Small things get really big results. Hold open a door for a colleague. Bring in an extra lunch in case someone you work with forgets theirs. Never speak ill of your colleagues. You will find that by just being you, a good person, your social capital will grow.

Time is the compounding interest that builds your social capital bank account. During your long career, there will be plenty of times for you to contribute important ideas that will benefit the school. Waiting patiently for those opportunities is essential.

When you feel the need to speak out in a meeting, don't do it until after you check in privately with others first. Aside from birthdays, no one really likes surprises. Before you go public with an idea, run it by three to four colleagues first. Ideally, you should approach the staff's biggest naysayer for an opinion. Listen to the other side. You can even manipulate the system by asking a trusted connector colleague to present your idea. If it benefits the school, do you really need the credit? Adjust your idea to be inclusive. In other words, by the time you present your idea at a staff meeting, everyone knows what is coming. Keep in mind that it is easier for people to say "no" and be dismissive than for them to be open to change.

In this particular meeting, after turning away from the cold stares and rethinking your idea, you decide to pack it in. Be patient, and take time to build your social capital.

➜ WHAT WILL YOU DO NEXT?—P. 27

4. Working One-on-One with a Colleague

IN any school, collaboration happens in many forms. Specific school issues can necessitate the creation of inquiry groups. Grade-level meetings are quite common, as are department-level meetings. In the most cohesive staffs, a core of teachers from across the spectrum of academic disciplines form a "team" and share the same students.

Getting the gears for collaboration started can be imposed top down from the administration or percolate up from the staff. Chances are, if forming collaborative working groups is promoted within your school, there will most assuredly be staff time set aside for a "first meeting" with your new working group.

The first day of teaming can be set up in several ways.

"I was told we need to collaborate." You turn around to see the face of a person you don't even recognize. You thought you knew every staff member, but who is this person? How can you build something with someone you barely even know?

Another opening: "I was told we need to collaborate." You gasp. Really? You? Before you even started working at your new job, you had heard about the teacher you are facing right now. This teacher goes through student detention slips like air. You feel like one of his students as you gasp for air. How can you work with someone who seems to hate his job, and you are up at bat?

Or: "I was told we need to collaborate." Bonus! The rockstar teacher on campus just reached out to shake your hand. This is going to work. You can grow and thrive—or can you? She is used to running her own show. Will there be enough room for the two of you on the stage?

Or then again: Silence. You look around the staff meeting. It seems as though everyone is comparing student lists and pairing off like they are getting ready for Noah's Ark. Everyone but you. How do you do the reaching out?

Throughout all of these scenarios, your focus needs to be on emapathy. Every person wants opportunities to shine and be appreciated. Even though teaching is a giving industry, don't forget that everyone has an ego. Most of all, don't forget to never lose perspective—kids' needs come first.

In collaborating with another teacher, how will you choose to facilitate collegiality? You:

1. Examine why students love your colleague but not you—p. 34

2. Persuade a colleague to collaborate as a team—p. 37

3. Get ideas from the principal about the stages in team development—p. 39

4. Examine why students love you and can't stand your colleague—p. 40

5. Advocate for collaboration—p. 41

6. Set the groundwork for collaboration through introspection—p. 41

7. Handle students who don't want to work with you—p. 43

8. Handle a colleague who tries to convince you to let a new teaming mandate pass—p. 44

Following is a discussion of each option. You can move from one to the next, or you can jump between options at any time.

Option 1. Examine Why Students Love Your Colleague but Not You

AS the school year starts, you begin team teaching with Ms. Patel. Students apparently adore her, and after two weeks have passed, you being to tire of hearing your students groan and mumble, "Ms. Patel doesn't do it like that" and "This class sucks. Is it almost over?"

You now end every day with one thought: "What am I doing wrong?" You know that effective self-reflection is essential for effective teaching, but you don't know where to start. You decide to breathe and contemplate your classroom. Some points start to rise in your mind:

1. How empathic am I to my students' lives?
2. Have I offered students an appropriate level of academic rigor?
3. Am I communicating with students and their families in a positive manner?
4. What is the structure of my classroom? Can students accurately predict what is expected from them on a daily and weekly basis?
5. Is my instruction in a rut? Is my approach too basic?

Because students agree that Ms. Patel's class is great, you decide to talk to her and ask if you can observe her class. First, though, you decide to run this idea by your principal. In that way, you will be showing him that you are interested in pursuing both collaboration and ongoing professional development.

If you have the same preparatory class as Ms. Patel, you need to get your class covered while you observe hers. You decide to check in with her first:

"Thank you for allowing me to see you in action," you say as you enter Ms. Patel's room after school.

"I'm glad you feel comfortable reaching out," she replies.

"I just feel as though I'm not doing my best work," you confess, "and I don't want a year like this." Once you have said these words, you feel a weight lift from your shoulders. This is real gamble on your part; no one wants to appear vulnerable. Your colleague's response now will be a reflection of her true character. Shunning or ridiculing you will indicate that she does not have a collaborative spirit.

"I felt the same way when I started out," she confides. You have more courage than I did. Reaching out to improve your game is rough and admirable." You are now much more at ease with your colleague.

She begins to outline what you will see in her class: "In the next ten minutes, I'll preview for you what I plan on covering. I want you to watch for student engagement. Once they are involved and interested, the content and skill enhancement will just flow in."

You can see her thinking sharpen as she articulates what she expects from her students. Your students. Your team's students. Your reaching out to Ms. Patel has created the beginning of The Team.

Ms. Patel checks her watch before saying, "We need to do this again after you observe me to make sure I followed through and actually did what we talked about."

You now feel more energized than before. Your talk with Ms. Patel has reinforced the importance of communication and camaraderie to true collaboration. You vow to make time for more ten-minute conversations with her. After talking to your principal again, you ask some of your fellow teachers if they will cover your class from time to time so you may have those conversations.

Once your classroom is covered, you come back to observe Ms. Patel implementing the plan you just discussed. First, Ms. Patel greets students at the door. You see that she is sizing them up even before they enter the room. Her focus is on one student with sagging shoulders and teary eyes. She simultaneously whispers some comforting words to that student while greeting the rest of the class as they enter the room. Individual attention has already taken center stage and the bell hasn't even rung yet. You see students running to her class. They are used to seeing her in the hall. They are used to her reaching out and caring. Students are personally invested. They don't want to let her down. She has already written the opening quick-write prompt on the board, so as students walk in, there is something for them to do.

You pull up a chair in the back of the room and you hear students' verbal jabs, such as "Why are you here?" Ms. Patel glides over and interrupts. "No. This is a team effort. We treat everyone with respect. I taught you better than that." Her subtlety strikes you on many levels. With "no," she has set limits. When she reminded students that "This is a team effort," she demonstrated thinking beyond herself. She emphasized social standards when she said, "We treat everyone with respect." And finally, she personalized her words by saying, "I taught you better than that." You realize that word choice and framing conversations matter more than you think.

After the bell rings, she continues to work the room. She has already worked the hallway. The teary-eyed student is composed, in class, and focused. Everything she does is subtle and forthright. She never stands in one place as she is giving instructions. The desks are arranged so that there are open lanes, providing fluid access to any desk in fewer than four strides.

During her initial instruction, her body orientation adjusts to her audience. Because you share many of the same students, you know many of these students' strengths and weaknesses. When she needs to make a critical instructional point, she is looking at the student who has the shortest attention span. Her ability to check for clarity on the fly is amazing. You see that her eyes seem to be everywhere—looking down on their work, watching the clock, and, most of all, on the students. During her ten-minute presentation, you never hear her yell across the room. If there is a disruption, her body is right next to the student who is acting out.

You never hear her reprimand a student. Instead, you hear the opposite: "Great job." "I like your focus." "You already know the answer to that question. I believe in your ability to think critically."

Even when she calls on students for answers, she goes beyond simply calling them by name. She routinely says, "The hard-working student in the back." "I'm not going to call on you because I know you know the answer. Let's get everyone involved." "I haven't heard your voice in too long. I know you have good insights to add." None of this seemed fake or contrived. Facilitating inclusion dominated the lesson.

After watching her, you think of the five questions you asked yourself about your teaching and applied them to Ms. Patel:

1. **How empathic is Ms. Patel to students' lives?**
   Clearly, her constant goal is to lower students' emotional barriers, otherwise known as *affective filters*. Reaching out to students and personalizing teaching orientation on the fly makes it clear that her empathy for her students drives her instruction.

2. **Has she offered students an appropriate level of academic rigor?**
   Academic rigor doesn't occur in extra-credit questions at the end of a weekly test. Rigor lives in scaffolding students up to a higher-level conversation and expecting them to reach that level. When Ms. Patel called on a student who didn't know an answer, she assured him, "You can pass on answering this question, but I will come back to ask you what you heard another student say." And she followed through, holding every student accountable to contribute to the class discussion. Making room for every voice to matter in the conversation models the expectation that every student matters. What is amazing is the way she differentiated her

instruction for each student while maintaining academic rigor for each one. For one of the special education students, she quietly said, "I'm going to call on you in two minutes with this question." She was able to maintain a high level of rigor on an individual basis because of her knowledge of her students.

3. **Does Ms. Patel communicate with students and their families in a positive manner?**

While Ms. Patel was doing her loop around the classroom, you could see her signing agendas. What else does she do? This is a key follow-up question.

4. **What is the structure of the classroom? Can students accurately predict what is expected from them on a daily and weekly basis?**

Obviously, the predictability level was high in her room. Students knew to be on time. Students knew what to work on when they entered. Most of all, there was the implicit trust. Students knew Ms. Patel would give them structured time to interact and demonstrate guided practice because of her consistency in instructional practice. Therefore, class disruptions were nonexistent.

5. **Is the instruction in a rut? Is Ms. Patel's approach too basic?**

How does she change her approach? A ten-minute glimpse isn't enough. Once again, this is a key follow-up question.

The epiphany hits you: Once you focus on students' needs first and create connections to them, you won't have to waste time on behavior consequences. Ms. Patel runs her room with constant positive behavior management. As she said, "I want to catch you doing things right."

Being open to new ways to teach has additional professional rewards. Once you show your willingness to grow as a teacher, if Ms. Patel is worth her salt, she will ask for feedback. Now you have a professional relationship cooking. The free flow of ideas strengthens both of you as teachers. Ultimately, you find that when you lower your own affective wall and observe doing the art of teaching well, you are more motivated to elevate your own practice. You realize that you are not competing about who can teach better. Collaboration enables you to elevate your own game.

Now that you have seen how easy it is to forge professional bonds with a colleague, you decide to reach out to other staff members, including support staff. You will follow these guidelines for yourself as you approach others:

1. Honesty: You are open to growth, so you need to have the courage to examine what you are good at and where you need to improve.

2. Non-defensiveness: Isn't being comfortable in your own skin what you want to model for your students? Why be defensive when your job is really about reaching out to students? The central question is how can you improve your work so students can thrive? Once you shift your focus away from beating yourself up, you can model the thriving nature you expect out of your students.

3. Asking questions: True professionals seek opportunities to improve their practice and do not waste time in self-defeating thinking.

→ WHAT METHOD WILL YOU TRY NEXT?—P. 33

Option 2. Persuade a Colleague to Collaborate as a Team

YOU are two months into the school year. You have started to set up your routine in your classroom. Your students' morale is high. You have already called all of your students' parents. It feels as though you are managing your new teacher existence well—except in one area. You still don't feel as though you have forged any real connection with Mr. Chen, the teacher with whom you share students. You decide that this will be your next focus, and one day after school, you knock on his door. Going in, you try to keep in mind that, for a litany of reasons, not everyone will unconditionally like you or want to work with you. The last thing you want is to get caught into squabbles with colleagues. Framing any team discussion around an attitude of appreciation will give you the most mileage towards modeling the collaborative behavior you want out of children.

There are multiple bonuses to teaming that go beyond the classroom. Teaming enables teachers to diversify their skill sets. Prime staff development opportunities abound when teachers teach other teachers. Communication skills and empathy development flourish when teachers teach each other. Teaming defeats isolation, which is a major cause of teacher alienation and burn out. Teaming embraces the totality of life. New people. New perspectives. New skill-base development. New life opportunities.

"Hey, do you have a minute?" you ask, as you peer into his classroom. He is busy weeding through student notebooks and entering grades on his computer.

"Not really. What's going on? What do you need help with?" he says impatiently.

"I don't really need any help. I just wanted to say hi. If this is the wrong time, I can come back."

"Yeah." He has already lost interest in talking with you as he looks back to his screen. "We'll talk another time."

As you slink out of the door, your mind reels with options:

1. Do nothing. Spend the year focused, as you should, on your students and developing your curriculum.
2. Be a nag. How many times do you have to try to start a conversation before you are seen as a mosquito that will not fly away?
3. Wait him out. Obviously Chen hasn't been sold on the value of collaboration. His focus is the work at hand. If you wait him out, you'll be left out in the cold.
4. Invest. Make an appointment with him to sell him on the idea of collaboration. In the same way you invested time in your students and their families, you need to invest in Mr. Chen to see dividends.

You start to unpack why you think collaboration is worth the investment. Above all, it helps students. Students get a unified message about work habit expectations; knowledge of students and parental outreach; and ideally, with highly functioning teaming, teachers present complimentary content.

First, presenting unified work habit expectations helps students to not waste time trying to figure out the logistics of navigating the classroom. Every teacher has his or her own behavior expectations for students—from how to enter, to how to sharpen a pencil, to how to ask for help, and the list goes on. If teachers overtly teach an aligned framework of how the classroom is run, students will be able to get to learning quicker. Transparency will enable parents to understand the logistics of how their children are being taught. Referrals to the main office will have deeper validity, because the main office will know the steps that led to the referral being the last resort in setting limits for a student. Most of all, teamed teachers know when the other teacher assigns work, so students are powerless to pit one against another.

Second, a teaching team that centers on knowledge of students and parental outreach is a team that helps all students thrive. Too often parents are yo-yos going back and forth to a school for individual teacher conferences instead of talking directly to all of the stakeholders in the child's education. Adults who invest the time to know each student's academic and personal histories are the adults who make the biggest impact in students' social and academic performance.

Third, teaming teachers present complementary content. Because neural pathways depend on schemas based on thematic trends, it is only logical to show common threads in instructional content. The logic behind cause-and-effect relationships are the same for math as it is for the scientific method, as it is for historical themes, as it is for writing persuasive essays, as it is for understanding kinesthetics in physical education, as it is in developing musical patterns and integrating the arts. Teaming can highlight the themes in content so students can decode the complexities of the world around them. The more teachers team and develop each other's understanding of each discipline's academic content, the more connections can be made, and the more easily effective instruction can be nurtured. In addition, our world is not divided into discreet academic disciplines. We continually meld together core elements from every element of our education to make sense of and thrive in our world.

With newfound vigor in your teaming philosophy, you decide to approach Mr. Chen again. You choose option number 4 and invest in developing a partnership.

"Hey, did you get my e-mail?" You walk into Mr. Chen's class at the end of the day. You find him packing his briefcase with what looks like two hour's worth of grading.

"Yeah. I didn't open it. Is this important? I'm pretty busy." Mr. Chen still will not look in your direction. You remind yourself to not take his actions personally. You just haven't earned his attention yet.

"Yeah, this is important," you respond with more self-assurance than you thought you had when you planned what you were going to say. You need him to buy into the concept of teaming. To develop a meaningful partnership, both you and Mr. Chen need to be invested. Your words may change, but the degree of your empathy cannot waver. Starting anything of meaning takes time and needs to be mutual.

"Yeah, this is important," you repeat. "We share the same students. I know I'm new to collaboration, but the more I think about it, the more we need this. We can make each other's lives easier. I'm hesitant to try anything new, just as you may be. But I would like to have a conversation for ten minutes so we can see if this could be a good fit. If you need to go, I understand, but I have ten minutes right now if you could hear me out."

The ball is in his court. "How can this help me?" Mr. Chen looks at you for the first time.

You have your in. Now to articulate all of your reasons for collaboration and keep the conversational ball in play.

→ WHAT METHOD WILL YOU TRY NEXT?—P. 33

Option 3. Get Ideas from the Principal About the Stages in Team Development

TEAMING is getting nowhere. You decide now is the time to get the principal's help. You end up knocking on her door soon after school has let out for the day. She appears to be busy, but she stops to talk to you.

"I need your help," you say. "My team partners and I are flat. We get along alright, but none of our conversations go in depth about student learning needs. I think there is more that we could do, but I don't know how to get there." Your honesty and openness feels good. Now instead of reprocessing what you said to make sure it sounded the way you wanted it to, you consciously make sure to be in the moment and listen.

Your principal's mouth forms a wry smile, "It is still early in the year. Be patient. Any relationship that is worthwhile is worth waiting for. Just because you are eager to partner at a deeper level doesn't mean your partner or your students are ready.

"There are four distinct levels of team integration. An outstanding resource for your own reading is Deborah Mackin's interpretation of team development, *The Team-Building Tool Kit,* which comes from B. W. Tuckman's work on how to help teams thrive. According to Mackin, there are specific stages to team building. Currently, your fledgling team is in its 'Forming Stage.' You are still trying to figure each other out. You are still working at a superficial level. No one wants to offend anyone else. Building trust takes time and patience and shouldn't be rushed.

"In a few months, once your comfort level rises, your team will enter the 'Storming Stage.' Jockeying for social status will be the primary obstacle you will face at this stage. You will probably want to quit your team at this point. Personality differences will crop up. You will lose sight of why teaming is important. This is the point when you should come back for administrative help. At this stage, you and your partner will need to be honest with each other and, most important, receptive to each other's strengths and weaknesses. No one is perfect, but by working together you can get closer to creating an optimal working environment for all students.

"Once you make it through the 'Storming Stage,' and I'm confident you will, your team will enter the 'Norming Stage.' Your team may lapse back into bickering and re-establishing personal boundaries. It will probably feel as though you are working in fits and starts. The payoff is that you will experience a closer, more authentic working relationship than before. Your openness to practical feedback on your instructional practice will make you a stronger professional. Your ability to provide insights to your partner will buttress his or her practice. Overall, this is the moment when your team will come into its own and be on the cusp of flourishing.

"This leads to a new level of day-to-day excellence. Once your team gets to the 'Performing Stage,' watch out. Your team will be the model. You won't remember a time when you succeeded without a team. You will seek your team partner during the passing periods to check in. Moment-by-moment open communication about student progress will be your norm. Because of that open communication, students will experience exponential personal, social, and academic growth. Soon you will look at data and find ways to reach more and more students. Just like everything else in life, the more time you invest, the greater your long-term payoff.

"So this is what you have to look forward to," she finished. "This is our district's vision and my vision for what we can be as educators and as a school."

You try to absorb your principal's foresight. It sounds like an arduous journey but a fun one. What is the use of living if you are not open to growing?

"So what is your next step?" Your principal challenges you. "Are you up to continue the conversation with your colleague?"

→ WHAT METHOD WILL YOU TRY NEXT?—P. 33

Option 4. Examine Why Students Love You and Can't Stand Your Colleague

YOUR team partner walks straight into your classroom without even knocking. "What are you doing in your classroom with the students we share?" he says. "The students can't stop talking about you. No matter what I do, all I hear is, 'Our other teacher does things better,' and 'We did this last year.' Worst of all, 'When is this class period over?'"

You are taken aback. Everyone told you the first year of teaching was going to be brutal. Maybe you have been overpreparing. Maybe your pre-teaching life experiences have enabled you to ease into this new life. Any way around it, you feel as though you are the only first-year teacher you know who is having a blast. Classroom disruptions are minimal. You have a beautiful rapport with your colleagues, administration, parents, and students. While everything isn't perfect, and you have had to stand your ground on a few occasions, overall, you feel as though you have your life under control.

How do you respond to this veteran colleague who is standing in front of you in your classroom? You team is still in the incubator mode. The last thing you want to be seen as is cocky or offensive. On the other hand, some of your students have come right out to complain about the teacher you are looking at right now.

You respond, "I listen to students. I model the empathy I want students to demonstrate. When I have a problem with a student, I problem-solve with him or her to make sure the student has ownership over he or she did and has a way out. I brainstorm a common understanding of the problem and make sure students have a say in the solution. I look for connections. I stand in the hallway during passing periods. I phone their homes. I follow through on limit setting. From what I've seen, you are doing all of these things as well."

"Yeah, but why am I not getting the same results?"

Your partner's response was the one you wanted. Now you can have a conversation filled with substance, focused on students. "Which students do you feel as though you are not getting through to? I'm struggling with a few as well. I'm sure there is a lot of information you know that I don't. Do you have a few minutes to check in on how our students are doing?"

You just shifted the conversation from a party celebrating you to a collaboration session where everyone can improve. Your partner pulls up a chair. You grab your roll sheet and your binder of notes on each student.

Focusing the conversation on student needs, and what each teacher can do to help out students, is an essential element to team development. Soon you find the two of you laughing at the students' antics in your classrooms. Through the dialogue of what works with each student, you both find ways to improve your presentation styles. You make it a point to meet more often after school. This investment in your team partner can provide you a source of companionship, a sounding board, and most of all a unified front to help all students to thrive.

→ WHAT METHOD WILL YOU TRY NEXT?—P. 33

Option 5. Advocate for Collaboration

TWO often-repeated phrases from colleagues resonate in your head:

1. "We have the top test scores in the district. Why do we need to do anything more?"
2. "There is this group of students no one can reach, because they don't care. If their parents don't care, why should we? Year after year, the same students come up at staff meetings. We can't save everybody."

You know your peers' comments aren't benefitting the school. On the other hand, you agree with them on some level. As teachers, we are doing a lot! We are constantly juggling our students' social, cognitive, emotional, and physiological needs, our responsibilities to our community and our school district, and our own personal lives outside of school. It is difficult to reject the initial knee-jerk reaction to kick back and say, "Really, we need to do something more? Why?"

But which battles do you pick? How much do you actually believe in collaboration? Are you advocate enough to argue its benefit to one colleague? How about arguing to a group of colleagues, a group in which you are the only one speaking in favor of investing more energy you don't have into something no one at your school has done?

You decide to pause and look at the larger picture. What do you have to lose personally and what do you have to gain professionally by advocating for collaboration?

First, you may lose social status among the staff, being labeled a kiss-up or, worse, "not one of us." You may find you have very little administrative support for moving forward with collaborative efforts. And last, you could lose a lot of sleep by investing in these new efforts.

But you could gain so much more. In terms of social status, you could rise in the administration's eyes by promoting collaboration. You could find, then, more administrative support for your overall efforts. Collaborating with the right people might help you feel less isolated and overwhelmed, which means more sleep for you.

Ultimately, you have to make a decision that is right for you.

➔ WHAT METHOD WILL YOU TRY NEXT?—P. 33

Option 6. Set the Groundwork for Collaboration Through Introspection

LIFE is great—you think. Students are attentive to you in class and are cordial in the hallways. Your classroom management seems to be right on. No disruptions means no problems, right? But you can sense something is wrong. You can't quiet a nagging voice in your head: "Is this as good as it gets?"

You see other teachers joking with students in the hallways. Students seem to gravitate to these other teachers. A fluidity emanates from their interactions.

As you travel to work, you reflect on your life at school. Are other teachers really making connections that are eluding you? Are you mired in a delusional mirage that you have it all together, when, in fact, you don't?

Essentially, you feel as though you need to right your own ship before you reach out to collaborate. Since developing the art of teaching is such a personal endeavor, one does need a supply of confidence before opening up to colleague.

Stopping and watching other teachers, you find that the teachers who seem most at ease in their own skin are the ones who are joking with their students and who don't take themselves too seriously. You realize your social persona leads to the reactions you get. What is your mission as a teacher? Which of the following do you want to be?

1. **Skimmer:** You don't make waves. You show up. You check in. You do your job. You leave. Fundamentally, you get life satisfaction from other sources, because without depth of time investment in this job, there isn't any depth of satisfaction.

2. **Wave Maker:** It's your way or the highway. No one ever hired you as principal, but you act like one anyway.

3. **Jokester:** Life is fun and games. No one takes you seriously—why should you take this place seriously? You have tenure and nothing to lose.

4. **Grouchy:** You count the days to retirement.

5. **Oblivious:** I'm having a great year. Aren't you? All of my students are great. Aren't yours? Life is great. My rose-colored glasses make everything sparkle.

6. **Lifer:** You are fundamentally all of the above, but you are authentically *you*. You have no hidden agendas and are open to growth. You see teaching as a way to change lives, especially your own. You love what you do. The reality of the matter is that you are really just a teacher. You grade papers. You are the bad guy sometimes. You laugh and cry for your students. And you love your life.

You decide to invest your time into being a lifer.

Because you have a spine, you decide to limit the amount of time beating yourself up over contrived self-doubt and get to the source of the problem. After a night tossing and turning in bed, you wake up exhausted but with renewed purpose. You have a plan centered on openness, self-reflection, and facing the reality of your teaching.

Step 1. Look at the student data: You take an honest look at your roster and the data points you have collated so far in the year. Which students seem to be thriving? Which students are stagnating? Which students are immobilized? This is a hard conversation to have with yourself. Ultimately, you decide to put the number of students who are "with you" on your white board and circle it. When students ask you what the number is for, ignore them. This will give the number the aura of mystery you want. You respond to this query after a few days. "This is the number of students who I think have decided to thrive in my classroom. Can I increase the total by 1? Are you with me?"

Step 2. Film: You need an objective viewpoint of your classroom. You decide to bring in a video camera and film yourself. Make sure to ask the principal for permission beforehand, depending on school policy. When students ask you, tell them the truth. "I always want to improve what I am doing. This videotape will be only for me. Nothing I film will end up on the Internet." Initially, students may ham it up. You can position the video camera in the back of the room for the first few days and not even turn it on. Soon, students will forget it is there and revert to being themselves. The camera lens doesn't lie. Like it or not, you will probably find multiple instances of students checking their phones when your back is turned. This could be just a new way of passing notes or it could be something far more intrusive. Any way around it, you have more data to decipher so you can reflect and improve your teaching practice.

Step 3. Survey your students: This is an ideal sponge activity for times when you finish your instruction five minutes earlier than you had planned. Say to them, "I always want to improve my practice, so I want to honor your viewpoints—how can I best meet your needs?" No matter how hard it is, sit, listen and take notes. Do *not* respond.

A written student survey may be a more reliable tool (see page 69). That night you read over student comments. You decide to categorize the results into piles. Which students are thriving, stagnant, or struggling? The next day, you report back to students so they know that you do read what they write and their voices matter.

Step 4. Repeat: You find this circle of self-inquiry gives you substantial information to take to collaboration meetings. Having the courage to face your own hard truths enables you to model the self-reliance you want your students to exhibit.

With the courage to face your own teaching reality, you now feel as though you can contribute to a team.

The reality is that you will never be fully loved by every student. Teaching is a slow transformative marathon, for your students and for you. To be a life-long effective educator is to be someone who is never satisfied with getting by. Some wisdom mentioned previously bears repeating: the process of pursuing perfection is perfection itself. The more you embrace being open to constant improvement, the less scary the life of a teacher is.

→ WHAT METHOD WILL YOU TRY NEXT?—P. 33

Option 7. Handle Students Who Don't Want to Work With You

ONE of your colleagues confronts you in the hallway. "I've already told other people, so I might as well tell you: your field trips are completely messing up my classes. You are taking the students we share away from my instructional time. What is the value in what you are doing?"

Handling co-workers effectively can be a roll of the dice. When should you stand your ground? When should you cave? How do you predict how your actions will resonate into tomorrow? Next week? Next semester? You don't know who talks with whom yet. The last thing you need is be mired in school politics.

You have heard about this colleague's negativity, which radiates though the staff. At the previous staff meeting, all she could talk about was how students and parents don't care, so why should she? Retirement cannot happen soon enough for this person.

So you decide to stand strong and stay away from making anything personal. "I want to broaden opportunities for all students to stretch themselves beyond our school doors," you reply. "Not only did I schedule my yearly plan months ago, we talked as a staff about collaboration. If you wish, I will gladly sit down with you and our principal to hear your concerns."

Your goal in you response was multifaceted. Stand your ground; stay away from making anything personal; focus on the needs of the community you serve; give the other person a way out. Ultimately, if you are in the right, you have nothing to apologize for. If you are serving the needs of students well, don't shy away from staying focused on your mission to best help the community—which, after all, is the focus of your job.

> ## Empathy Break
>
> Never forget that every person who teaches starts out wanting to do well and does care about helping others. The grind of time and the disappointment of non-fulfillment can make even the most optimistic person bitter and resentful.

You remember that negativity is a virus and you don't want to be contaminated. You will only end up inadvertently spewing out the hatred onto your own students, or worst of all, the people you love outside of school. Your best solution is simply to quarantine your viral-host colleague by setting boundaries. When you interact with her, you are determined to be cordial and friendly, but you don't have to be friends. You have to be okay with not being friends with everyone. Rick Patino, one of the greatest basketball coaches of all time is fond of saying, "Four things I've learned in my fifty-nine years about people. I ignore the jealous, I ignore the malicious, I ignore the ignorant, I ignore the paranoid" (CBSSports.com 2011). As a teacher, or as a human being, you don't want to appear to be in any of these four categories. Listen to your fellow teacher, but most of all, never burn bridges. This will always backfire. You have no idea if and when you will ever need to ask this colleague for help with something. If a bridge is ever burned, let the other person carry the torch—while you carry a raft to row back across and save them.

→ WHAT METHOD WILL YOU TRY NEXT?—P. 33

Option 8. Handle a Colleague Who Tries to Convince You to Let a New Teaming Mandate Pass

THE first team collaboration time has arrived. You look forward to it and want to know how it works. Thankfully, you are paired with a veteran teacher, who can guide you. However, you feel your optimism evaporate within the first five seconds of sitting down with your partner.

Being genuine and making eye contact the entire time, your "partner" throws verbal cold water on your vision. "I'll meet with you," she begins cooly. "You seem like a nice person. I'm open to hanging out. But this is just another program being pushed on us from the administration and the district office to substantiate someone's job. What I do works. I know it works because I see it work. My students may not get the highest test scores, but who cares? I teach what I know students need to learn to do well in school and in life. So yes, we should meet when they tell us to, but I'm going to bring my grading."

So what do you do? How do you engage someone who has no interest in it? You can run through your pro arguments about the value of teaming, but you know full well you will just be dismissed as a green-behind-the-ears-whippersnapper-know-it-all.

Unfortunately, in most school districts your dismissive colleague would be completely correct. It is too common for school districts to shift from one "new program" to another "new program," when everyone in teaching knows each of these fads comes and goes. As you listen to other teachers, you hear comments that are all variations on the same theme. "This will all blow over." "Who has the time to do this?" "They'll just have a new grand plan next year."

With only twenty-four hours in a day, there isn't enough time to do all of the things teachers already want to do and are expected to do. Where should a veteran teacher get the motivation to latch onto a "new idea" when all of the ideas have already fluttered by?

You have so many plans for collaboration. Good plans. You have already learned through your own life experiences that there is nothing there with this colleague.

You decide to play your only cards—patience and relationship building. Nothing can replace face-to-face relationship building. You listen and watch. You and your partner spend the time allocated for teacher team collaboration getting to know one another. In some meetings, all you say is a conversation starter: "What are some of the other fads you have seen come and go?" or "If you could fix anything at this school, where would you start?" or "How have students changed over the time you've been teaching?"

Collegiality quickly follows. A comfort level builds between the two of you, mostly because you didn't force yourself on your partner. Patience rocks.

Over time, you start to offer suggestions. The turning point is when you convince your colleague to spend time with you outside of school, going for drinks or a meal. Even walking during lunch can do the trick. You slowly guide the team-building times from conversations about yourselves to conversations about students. Ideally, by mid-point in the year, you two have started to coordinate your curricular planning so assignment due dates don't often overlap. You look at student data together and start to shore up your collective approach. A breakthrough moment comes when you find places where you can work off of each other's strengths to fine-tune your teaching approaches so all students can thrive.

You feel victorious as your partner starts the teaming conversation at lunch. But this is not the only way teaming can go.

→ WHAT METHOD WILL YOU TRY NEXT?—P. 33

5. Back-to-School Night

NOW that you have started your relationships with your students, it is time to begin building your relationships with the families. Tonight is Back-to-School Night at your school. You know that this initial meeting with the parents will frame conversations about you around kitchen tables and during car rides in the coming year.

You liken building a relationship with students and parents to building a home:

- Foundation—Foundation
- Structure—Walls
- Permanency—Disaster-resistant structural supports
- Honesty—Windows
- Warmth—Insulation
- "Extra Mile"—Decorative touches

Using the metaphor of a house helps you to clarify and communicate your teaching values. You explain that the foundation you want is for students to develop the desire and courage to take academic and social risks. The structure of your room will foster security. Conveying your consistency in routine, which provides limits and predictability, helps to ensure students have a safe harbor in your classroom. The walls of your metaphorical house and your real classroom enable students to feel secure enough to be advocates in their own academic and social growth.

Despite your best plans, something will always go wrong, so it's important to offer students permanency, or dependability. The best way to do this is through open communication. The wider community needs to know you are accessible to help these students.

Next comes honesty. What are the metaphorical windows the wider community will use to see into your work? After working with you, how will you change your students' vision of the wider world through the metaphorical windows of your teaching? Once again, you decide your teaching needs to be value-driven. Inclusivity, openness, responsibility, and kindness all need to ring true to what you do.

Insulating students from the trials of the real world does not serve their best interests. Conversely, students need to be warm to thrive. How will you convey to students and parents that you want to foster independence but still keep students "warm and dry?"

Last, extra touches mean a lot to people. What is the "extra mile" that you can go to make parents comfortable with your presence in students' lives?

Now that you have your values in place, how do you effectively communicate these priorities for Back-to-School Night?

How do you navigate other obstacles on your big night? You:

1. Are cornered by a parent for a conference—p. 48
2. Confuse two students when you talk with a parent—p. 49
3. Run out of time for what you want to say—p. 50
4. Give a model teacher presentation—p. 50
5. Talk at parents and read your syllabus—p. 52
6. Answer a challenge to your empathy-based student-centered teaching philosophy—p. 52
7. Reach out to parents who don't attend Back-to-School Night—p. 54
8. Have students present while you act as their coach—p. 54

Following is a discussion of each option. You can move from one to the next, or you can jump between options at any time.

Option 1. A Parent Corners You for a Conference

YOU have just finished giving your presentation. You have a few moments left, so you decide to "work the crowd." Face-to-face contact trumps any other communication connection. Many parents express their appreciation of your phone calls earlier in the year. You are feeling quite good about how the night is progressing until you come across one parent, who is standing with arms folded and fists clenched.

"Do you have a minute?" she asks. Her voice grabs your attention, but you need to get ready for your next presentation.

"Um, I'd love to talk with you," you say, "but I have another set of parents about to enter the room. Is there another time we can talk?"

"No. Now," she insists. "You work for me. And I want your attention now. You don't understand what my child needs. The school year just started and already my son thinks he can't do anything right in your class. We've never had this experience before. What do you have against my son?" The pent-up anger radiates from her body, causing you to take a step backward.

Breathe, you tell yourself. Don't react. You do not even know whose parent this is, so you have no idea what problem she's talking about, but you know how upset she is. If you try to avoid her or brush by her, it will only make the situation worse. You look past her shoulder and see the incoming wave of parents of your next class, who also deserve your attention. You really need to make this conversation last only five seconds. The only way to pull this off is with honesty, compassion, and limits—just like you would treat any of your students.

"First of all, ma'am, I don't know who you are, but your concerns are a priority for me, just as all parents' concerns are. I have only a minute to listen to you now, but we can start our conversation. I want to make sure I am serving your family well. Before you leave, I want to put you on my calendar so we can finish the conversation."

The less you talk now, the more power you have. When you sincerely ask what the parent needs and invest your time in listening, you can dissect the issues and create bridges to a common solution.

She now has three different choices of responses:

1. Realize that she is in a public space, and schedule a meeting for a private conversation.
2. Not to back down, make a spectacle of herself, and confront you in front of everyone.
3. Walk away in a huff to talk with your principal.

Your response to all three must be the same: patience and compassion. Your primary job tonight is to introduce yourself to the world you will be working with for the next ten months. It will be a marathon course. You need to set the tone early that you will not jump at every reaction, nor will you ignore a parent's wish.

The confrontation with this parent and your necessary follow-through are not private encounters. Parents will compare notes about you and every other teacher. Hence, you must support this parent in getting her questions answered after you attend to your primary responsibilities of tonight.

➜ HOW DO YOU NAVIGATE THE NEXT OBSTACLE?—P. 47

Option 2. You Confuse Two Students When You Talk with a Parent

YOU get through all of the information you wanted to get through. It ends well. There is a heartfelt round of applause, and you still have time to schmooze and answer questions. A group of parents walks up to you.

You think you are demonstrating your best inclusivity and sensitivity. You turn and face a parent and start a conversation, "Your son has had an outstanding start to our school year." Unfortunately, you have struck up a conversation with the wrong family.

The parent responds, "I think you have confused me with someone else. My daughter is enrolled in your class."

"Um . . . I'm terribly sorry," you mutter. Now parents are staring at you.

Knowing she has the attention of other parents, the parent you attempted to talk with begins to dress you down: "You just spent your Back-to-School presentation trying to convince us that you care about building relationships between home and school. Do you even know my daughter's name? Do you genuinely care, or are you just going through the motions? How invested are you in our children?"

A sea of expectant eyes awaits your response. What could you possibly say to save face—your face?

You decide to fall back on your baseline of integrity (using I statements to own your actions), compassion (demonstrating sympathy—no parent wants to be taken for granted), and professionalism (paving the way to move forward).

"I am very sorry for my gaffe. I am also sorry if I gave you the impression that I don't know my students. Of course I know them. I have begun the yearlong process of fostering academic proficiency through building personal relationships with all students. I see students as more than just a series of test scores. Understanding as much as I can about each student's individual needs and histories enables me to teach the full person. That is why I have already called every child's home. How would you like to move forward so we can collaborate to best provide for your daughter's growth?"

You can see shoulders lower as you wait for the parent's response. You have been successful in making the jump from rookie defensiveness to veteran security in not having to prove yourself.

You make a mental note that the parents who make the biggest social scenes are the most insecure. Perhaps this parent is hurting and feeling out of touch with her child. Extra patience is the best solution with this family. Regardless of how this parent reacts to your question about moving ahead, the wisest thing you can do is call that home—tonight—ideally before 8:30 p.m. Stay consistent in powering forward. Instead of rehashing the misunderstanding, all you will need to say is, "Is this a bad time for me to call? Thank you for coming to Back-to-School Night. Is there anything else you wanted to talk about?"

Obviously, you will keep a written record of all of your parent telephone calls, including dates and times of the calls. Part of being professional is to protect yourself in case of any parental backlash. Any parent who would try to embarrass you in front of other parents would complain about you to the principal in a heartbeat. Don't let this interaction cloud your service to their child.

→ HOW DO YOU NAVIGATE THE NEXT OBSTACLE?—P. 47

Option 3. You Run Out of Time for What You Want to Say

PARENTS are about to meander out of your room, but you have covered only half of what you wanted to say. You feel a little panicked.

You stop and try to collect yourself. You remind yourself to breathe.

Since you teach multiple classes, you decide to recalibrate and redraw your attention to the next group of parents who are queuing up to enter your classroom.

You look back at your notes. You have only a set amount of time to convey your teaching philosophy, values, and orientation to life. Another way to look at it is this: what do you think parents are really looking for at Back-to-School Night? People have been sizing you up all night based on how you dress, the angle of your shoulders, your handshake. You know that first impressions are very, very important.

That is the key element. Your composure tonight will set the tone for all of your future interactions. Flipping through your notes of what you want to cover tonight, you see where you lost time and can abbreviate your comments.

And you breathe.

→ HOW DO YOU NAVIGATE THE NEXT OBSTACLE?—P. 47

Option 4. Give a Model Teacher Presentation

The essential challenge of Back-to-School Night is this: how do you set a positive tone for your school year and generate collaboration with parents? Fundamentally, you need parents on your side. This is the start of a marathon year in which you need to invest and present yourself as the voice of reason in the chaos that could be education. You think to yourself, I want to make it clear that I am open but not a pushover, and that I care for the whole child, but my instruction must be about the standards. How do I do this?

You decide to start with your heart and try to interject humor. Just like when you teach, you know not to "wing it." During your first few years of Back-to-School Nights, you will need to script and rehearse what you say. You decide that for every one minute of practice time you spend, you will probably save ten minutes of parental cleanup work throughout the year.

You project a cartoon for parents to read as they wait for you to start your presentation. You position yourself at the door to greet parents, make eye contact, and shake hands. Comic strips such as Calvin and Hobbes, for Better or Worse, Zits, or Luann can provide treasure troves of examples of the plights of growing up and parenting.

When you present, you will need to cover the following issues:

1. Teaching philosophy: All students can and will do well
2. Overview of the year
3. How parents can help—being a support and having a team mentality
4. Open communication fosters a team mentality.
5. Include the invitation-only events—something to strive for. (See p. 79.)

As you script out your talk, you are bound to come up with some fantastic lines that encompass all of your goals. Your talk may sound something like this:

"Thank you so much for investing the time to come in tonight. I will first cover this course's academic and character development goals. I'm looking forward to helping to bring out the best in every child. To do this, I will try to be as direct and open as possible so that you know exactly what is going on in your child's life in our classroom.

"My overarching teaching philosophy is to foster an environment where all students can thrive and grow socially as well as academically. Over the next month, I will confer with each student to come up with common goals for the school year. The purpose behind these conferences is to personalize the academic goals outlined in the syllabus and set social goals as well. That is why I called each of your homes already, to solicit parental perspectives in the formulation of students' objectives."

Step 1 is now done. You have framed your perspective, so you can refer to your syllabus. But as you do this, be sure to talk about the invitation-only events you have planned for the course of the year. An invitation-only event is a culminating one-class-period lesson during which students apply the content they learned in your classroom. The invitation-only element is critical. Students will need to do the actual work to earn the privilege of participating in these events.

Now, Step 2 and Step 5—overview of the year, and invitation-only events—are done.

Before you close your presentation, make sure you let your audience know that your classroom door is open. You will need parents and guardians on your side. After you give an overview of your year, you may want to hand out a parent skill survey. While you are presenting, pass around a list of how parents can help in the classroom based on your instructional goals. Specifically, if you are putting one of the fictional characters on trial to highlight persuasion and motive—why not bring in a parent who is a lawyer? Or if you are covering the Renaissance, why not bring in a parent who is an aspiring inventor, scientist, or computer programmer to discuss the creative and scientific process? Conversely, if you are covering the Great Depression, you can bring in any parent who has ever successfully or unsuccessfully looked for a job. The intent behind this twist to parent inclusion is not to have a revolving door of guest speakers, but to create a list of connections for your students to contact for surveys, experiential exercises, and other well-rounded research that goes beyond Internet searches. You will find that regardless of where or what you teach, there will be a wealth of community resources that you may not have been aware of. You will need to brainstorm your curriculum beforehand to create a volunteer list that effectively correlates to your year objectives.

You will also need to show empathy for how parents think about boundaries and goals. This can best be summed up with a few compassionate statements like this: "I know parents live and breathe for their children. Parents naturally want to protect, inspire, and nurture their child's development. Ultimately though, a parent's goal is to get the child out of your house. We want to develop community-minded, independent, thoughtful, compassionate people. Working together to maintain open communication so we can support each other in limit setting will be essential. This is a team effort." With this welcoming yet straight-forward attitude, you take care of Step 3, how parents can help, and Step 4, open communication.

➡ HOW DO YOU NAVIGATE THE NEXT OBSTACLE?—P. 47

Option 5. You Talk at Parents and Read Your Syllabus

YOU can fake enthusiasm, but at your core you have dreaded Back-to-School Night. You decide that you are just going to read your syllabus. Everything you need to say is on the syllabus. You convert it to a PowerPoint® for expediency. You have made a plan, which leaves no time for questions and answers.

During your presentation, you talk about the scope and sequence of the curriculum you will be covering. You have included a slide for your grading policy. You even gave a long list of materials you think every student should have. In your head, you did your job.

Unfortunately, your job encompasses more than just PowerPoint® slides or a syllabus. You have already experienced some problems in your classroom:

1. Students either don't finish their homework on a consistent basis or they cheat.
2. A number of students are consistently late or truant.
3. Students act out in your class.
4. You have seen multiple indicators that other staff members and the administration don't take you seriously.

Your brain searches for connections and comes back to the same refrain, "You get out of an event what you put into an event." What do you want students to learn? Just the content standards? Most people can grind out a year guiding students through a scripted curriculum where everyone should be on the same page at the same time. But if that's all you are going to put into your teaching efforts, you may not reap any great benefits. The act of reading off of your syllabus reflects the distance you want to maintain from a commitment to doing your job well. Consequently, parents do not take you seriously.

By confining yourself to teaching academics, you are inherently ignoring a driving force needed in education—modeling and nurturing students' character development. You muse over the social message you are conveying, that life is for just buckling down and getting through, instead of relishing and enjoying.

The bottom line is that, in a classroom, students rise to the level of commitment modeled by the head of the class. And the head of the class is you. If you focus on the academic requirements alone, you will never truly teach.

➡ HOW DO YOU NAVIGATE THE NEXT OBSTACLE?—P. 47

Option 6. Answer a Challenge to Your Empathy-Based Student-Centered Teaching Philosophy

YOU have just finished your presentation and you're feeling pretty good about your performance. "I have time to answer a few questions," you say. "Is there anything on your mind I didn't answer?"

You hear a voice from the back of the room: "I'm confused. You seem to be presenting two contrary goals. You want our students to be working at grade level with a vision for their future, but you won't be assigning that much homework. My daughter is behind in reading and math. How do you propose to bring her up to grade level without putting in the extra time? She needs to put in her 'ten thousand hours,' as you put it. Will this all be done at school?"

Remember, just because parents expect a quick response doesn't mean you need to jump when asked to jump. Before you respond, use your best negotiation skills:

Step 1. Identify the issue: This parent is not convinced his child will work hard enough in this classroom. Parents often measure their child's academic progress based on what they see at home. The fallacy in this thinking is that if the child is working on homework, then he or she is doing well in school, which does not always correlate.

Step 2. Respectfully correct the fallacy—standing your ground on your values will do nothing but benefit you as a person and as a professional.

Step 3. Give the parent a way out—Always leave the door open to further conversations.

Your brain quickly scans your mental notes of how school should be run. Thankfully you land on the perfect place—your empathy-based student-centered teaching philosophy influenced primarily by Denise Clark Pope (2001).

"My primary focus as a teacher is to teach relevant skills to our students. To do that, I will closely monitor all of my students' progress. Just because students aren't doing extra homework does not mean that they are not pursuing their ten thousand hours of mastery. Because school time in my classroom is optimized for instruction, homework for homework's sake is disrespectful of students' time and the diligence they displayed during school hours. Also, less homework leaves space for students to diversify their learning opportunities through arts, sports, community involvement, and so on. These opportunities don't need to cost money and are not necessarily additional clubs or structured activities. With video games and TV and Internet off, students can learn meaningful life skills in any environment by connecting to family members and community members. Everything should be in moderation. Less homework is not necessarily a bad choice.

"The purpose of homework is to reinforce skills, not teach new ones. Simultaneously, school should be the place where students learn new skills and information and not just show off what they already know. Homework needs to be meaningful. I don't want to create an environment where students just do school. Extra homework doesn't translate into increased ability. The only homework I assign will be meaningful."

Quite often, when you stand your ethical ground, parents won't know how to respond. You will hear about this encounter later, either via e-mail or worse, through the principal, because the parent thought you would not be approachable. Be patient and hold firm to your values.

As you go home after Back-to-School Night, you replay this encounter over and over again in your head. Later in their lives, your students will never be asked what their grades were in your class. Conversely, for the rest of their lives on a daily basis, either consciously or subconsciously, at some level they will emulate your positive and negative influences. With the weight of the social impact you will make every day as a teacher, you decide to be more resolute in your values of modeling respect for your students, their time, and their pursuit of academic excellence.

→ HOW DO YOU NAVIGATE THE NEXT OBSTACLE?—P. 47

Option 7. Reach Out to Parents Who Don't Attend Back-to-School Night

IF you work in a school where 100 percent of parents and guardians show up at any function, you should never cease to be thankful. If you work at one of the other 99.99 percent of schools, you still have a lot of work to do after Back-to-School Night to construct the bridge between students' work life and home life.

After everyone has left and you muse over your night, you start to pick apart the meaning behind Back-to-School Night. Is it a "dog and pony show?" Is the only goal to parade around and go through the motions of proving to them that you are honest and would like for parents to be involved? Or is it an opportunity to create a united front to help all students thrive? What you do after Back-to-School Night is the measure of your true commitment to bringing families into the fold of your educational program.

You decide to call the homes of those parents you did not meet at Back-to-School Night, and you plan what you are going to say before you even pick up a phone: "Hi. I'm calling because I missed seeing you last night at Back-to-School Night. I just wanted to let you know what we covered last night."

You keep two cautions in mind as you make the calls: First, you call only the homes of parents and guardians who weren't there. Calling the home of a parent who was there will be nothing but awkward. Second, you keep the calls short. You don't want parents to think you will be calling home every other week.

You rise above parents' apologies for not making it in. A quick, nonjudgmental "Everyone is busy and doing the best they can" comment can go a long way in reinforcing your reputation as the kind inclusive teacher you want to be.

➜ HOW DO YOU NAVIGATE THE NEXT OBSTACLE?—P. 47

Option 8. Students Present and You Act as Their Coach

YOU decide to try something novel that you have never seen: You will have your students run Back-to-School Night while you operate as a coach. The more you think this through, you more you outline your game plan:

- Honesty
- Organize your time
- Effectively delegate responsibilities
- Be comfortable with not being perfect
- Allow students to fail

1. **Honesty:** What are your fundamental goals for this night? The last thing you want is to be a circus ringleader and prance your students on the stage for show. If your students do present, it will have to be for a reason and not just to be cute. Your motivations for bringing your students to the spotlight instead of yourself will need to be clear. The only reason you would choose this option is to highlight how much you are trying to foster student leadership and engagement in your program. That is a good reason, so keep that idea at the forefront of what you are doing.

2. **Organize your time:** In many schools, there is a specific time constraint for Back-to-School Night. Rely on planning beforehand. What are the five key concepts you want parents to take home? In setting up and preparing students for their big night, you will need to reinforce

your collective goals over and over again. This is only to your own benefit. The best way to know anything thoroughly is to teach it. So what are the five key concepts you will center the presentation on?

    a. Teaching philosophy

    b. Overview of the year

    c. How parents can help

    d. Open communication fostering a team mentality

    e. Invitation-only events

You can close the evening with a parent skill survey. This will give the message that you are invested in including the entire family, which is ideal for any grade level.

3. **Effectively delegate responsibilities:** Two ideal formats for your students' presentation could be small groups as you circulate, or a fishbowl exercise. Small groups are doable and ideal. Parents and guardians can sit in small groups with two student leaders. Student leaders can have a "cheat sheet" outline of talking points you want covered. Ideally, you would have spent one class period creating an outline of Back-to-School Night objectives together with students. Fostering student ownership helps ensure more authentic and informed outcomes. Fishbowl exercises are similar to small-group presentations but in reverse. This option is a more promising and safer one than small groups. You can have three or four students discuss your class objectives between themselves while parents look in from the outside. If time permits, parents can ask questions after students finish discussing your class's preplanned objectives.

4. **Be comfortable with not being perfect:** This is probably the most important concept you should center your professional career around. Taking risks and being open to new ideas, which enable students to be leaders, can *never* be to your detriment. Yes—going with a small group or fishbowl model may fail horribly in conveying your Back-to-School message. In the larger picture, by modeling to the community and your students that you embrace new ideas and are willing to take on new ways of thinking, you will quickly be embraced as a fresh new voice in your school environment.

5. **Allow students to fail:** Failing does not equal humiliation. Failure looks like the information in your syllabus and how your run your class does not adequately conveyed. What does come across with this approach is that students' voices are valued. You decided early in your career to not embarrass students in social settings—especially in front of their loved ones. If you are going to have students present—yes, you are always responsible for your classroom. Simultaneously, you are also responsible for bringing out the best in your students. With appropriate reflection, everyone learns more from failure than from reinforcing success.

In your planning to implement this idea, you keep in mind that the next day you will need to debrief what went right and how to make this event better. During any effective debriefing, ask questions. Model the nonjudgmental air with which you would want to be treated. Compliment what went right, and do not scorn shortcomings. Most of all, focus on how thrilled you are that your students were bold enough to try something new.

→ HOW DO YOU NAVIGATE THE NEXT OBSTACLE?—P. 47

6. How to Work with a Recalcitrant Student

YOU noticed that Alex had a confrontational attitude on the first day of school, and you just attributed it to back-to-school jitters. It is now October and the middle of the day has become your dungeon of despair, all because of one student—or so you think.

Every day, periods one through three aren't bad—students can be downright delightful. Just last week you had a model lesson in which your students seemed almost thrilled to be in your room. However, as fourth period approaches, you start to shake.

As you are stand outside your classroom during the passing period, you can see Alex around the corner. You anticipate another class filled with eye-rolls and conspiratorial snickering. You hear your mentor teachers say, "Each day is a new opportunity. It is up to you to give each child a new chance to thrive each new day." But it is so difficult to let go of your frustration.

Alex dominates your time and attention. Either he is up out of his seat, sharpening his pencil for the three hundredth time that class period, or he is seated with his back to you, still talking about last Friday night even though it is Wednesday afternoon.

Nothing seems to work with this child. You have tried almost everything: after-class talks in which he won't make eye contact; changing his seat, where he just cultivates a new audience; and sending him to the main office—but you don't want to appear as though you can't control your own classroom. You have even tried the good-guy approach with positive reinforcement—it seems as though he doesn't hear it.

After another day of the same limit setting with Alex, you have had your fill.

What is your next move? You:

1. Speak to Alex's mother and she is nonplussed—p. 58
2. Speak to Alex's mother and she is cantankerous—p. 58
3. Use 'I' statements and empathy with Alex and his mom—p. 59
4. Consider becoming more Draconian with Alex—p. 60
5. Research Alex's school records and develop more empathy—p. 62
6. Change your pedagogical approach—p. 63
7. Call in the principal to mediate—p. 65
8. Opt out of confrontation and change Alex's schedule with no character development occurring—p. 65
9. Reach out to a trusted colleague for suggestions, promoting more collegiality—p. 66

Following is a discussion of each option. You can move from one to the next, or you can jump between options at any time.

Option 1. Alex's Mother is Nonplussed and Nothing Changes

"**H**I. I'm your son's teacher. Is this a good time for me to talk with you?" You wait for what seems like a long time for a response.

"This is as good a time as any," the mom says. You can feel the ice coming through your end of the phone line.

"I wish I was calling home with better news." You pause to let this sink in. It never occurs to you how many phone calls like this Alex's mother has received in her life. You think back. Unfortunately, this is the first time you can recall talking to her—ever.

"What's going on? What is this all about?" She sounds distracted and distant. Nonplussed. Noncommittal. You start to wonder why you are calling.

"Alex has been very disruptive in my classroom," you begin. "He is always pulling other students off-task. He rarely arrives on time and he is almost never prepared." This is not going the way you wanted. You feel as though you are coming across as whiney and accusatory.

Alex's mother's voice breaks through your thinking. "What I'm hearing you say is that you can't teach my son. So why are you calling me? What do you want me to do?"

"I was hoping you could talk to him. My attempts to reach out to him seem to have fallen flat."

"Sure," she says. "I'll talk to him when I get a chance." Before you can respond, you hear the line go dead.

The next day, Alex just stares at you as he approaches your classroom. Alex just walks right by you, ignoring your outstretched hand. He pauses before he enters your room to grind his heel on your shadow. Once the class period starts, you see that nothing has changed. Alex is just as off-task as ever and doubly rude.

➜ WHAT IS YOUR NEXT MOVE?—P. 57

Option 2. Alex's Mother is Cantankerous and Nothing Changes

YOU thought it would be a good idea to call home with Alex standing nearby. This is your lunch period, and you're hungry.

"Put my son on the phone!" yells his mom. The last thing you wanted was to get screamed at. What a horrible day this is turning out to be.

Alex is grinning at you as you hand the phone over to him. He snatches the phone from your hand. Victory is his. He knows it, and he is flaunting it.

"I know, mama. I know," he sneers. "Next year will be better with a new teacher." You want to run away, but this is your classroom.

How can you make it through this humiliation and regain some sense of order in your classroom? Undoubtedly, every child will now know you are beatable. Just get a parent to yell at you and you turn to jelly. How did this turn so negative? How can you salvage your social standing?

You find yourself in reactionary, damage-control mode. Rule number one is to survive the day. For the rest of the day, you are a zombie pretending to focus.

Breathe. As you drive home, you slowly replay the interaction again and again in your head. What did you do wrong? You called home to try to collaborate with the parent of a disruptive child. What is wrong with that?

Your misplay was your lack of connectedness with this family. All the parent knows is what Alex is telling her. Of course the parent is embarrassed and protective. The parent lives with Alex. The parent is the ultimate expert on Alex. Who are you to call home and say that their parenting is producing a noncompliant student? How have you invested time with the parent to build up your collateral? Was this your first phone call home? Have you reached out before? The only thing the parent knows is that you are a complainer. She's been living with Alex for years, and you can't handle a handful of days.

What do you know about Alex anyway? Yes, you have gone into this blind. No wonder it backfired. You need to do your research.

➜ WHAT IS YOUR NEXT MOVE?—P. 57

Option 3. Use 'I' Statements and Empathy with Alex and His Mom

YOU are ready to call Alex's parent to talk about his behavior. You think back to preschool, when you first learned how to use "I statements."

"Hi, I'm Alex's teacher," you start out, "I wish I were calling home with better news. I just had a very difficult time in class with your son. Is this a good time to talk? I just want your son to thrive in my class and I need your help."

"I can't tell you how thankful I am that you called me," says the mom. You exhale. It was the right thing to do to call home.

"I have had a really tough time with him over the past month. He always has a rough beginning to the school year. We think that he is just trying to impress other students. You know what happened to him last summer, don't you?"

The alarm bells go off in your head. Where is your binder in which you document parent telephone calls?

"Can you hold on for a moment, please?" You reach across your desk for your student information binder. Thank goodness you are organized. Alphabetized in your binder are three key pieces of information about each of your students: a student information sheet filled in by the child on the first day of school (see page 69); a picture of the child; and a writing sample from the second day of school. You review the paperwork as you continue talking to the mom.

You calmly review Alex's writing—rushed, superficial, and distant. He left several questions in his student information sheet empty: Who is your hero? What is your favorite thing you did this summer? Please describe your ideal life when you are twenty-five years old.

The jigsaw puzzle that is Alex is becoming more complete.

Empathy Break

Why does Alex lash out? He may be scared. Perhaps he can't conceptualize looking ahead to being twenty-five, and he might be petrified to look back.

So what is your next move with Alex? More punitive gestures? More stand-offs? Or more empathy? When have you been lost? When have you been scared? You start to think of how much class time Alex has wasted over the years posturing for the amusement of his peers and the disillusionment of his teachers. No wonder his skills are so low.

Alex arrives on time to class. You are so surprised that you don't know what to say. After a pause, you say, "It's nice to see you all today. Let's get to work." He is even sitting in his actual assigned seat— and, would you believe, facing you.

The class period feels "normal." You follow your plan. Your timing might be a little off; no one is perfect. But the biggest jaw-dropping surprise is that Alex is an active participant. He even raised his hand for clarification of your instructions.

You know that one day is a statistical anomaly. But then this same level of positive engagement goes on for a week, and you just have to check in with Alex.

You ask him if you could talk with him briefly during the passing period. You have a late pass in your hand so he doesn't get in trouble with his next teacher. "You seem to have a new attitude in class. I'm really glad. Could you tell me what has changed for you?"

He looks up at you, making eye contact. "I thought it over. You really aren't so bad. After you called home, my mom and I talked. Lots of teachers have called home before and made my mom cry. They would say really mean stuff about me. I guess I deserved it all. After all, school is usually lame. I'm just sitting there and listening all day. I need to do stuff, not just sit.

"Your phone call was different. Mom said you asked questions. You didn't tell her she was a horrible parent. You didn't make my mom cry. She said you cared. So I thought I would give you another chance."

A burst of pride swells inside your chest. You realize again that teaching is so much more than just delivering content. You are in the people business. You were a success on this one. Collaboration trumps finger-pointing every time. This teaching thing might work out after all. But how do you keep the positive vibe going?

➜ WHAT IS YOUR NEXT MOVE?—P. 57

Option 4. You Consider Becoming More Draconian with Alex

"I'M done. I'm done. I'm done," you intone to yourself after you hang up the phone with Alex's mom. "Wow, that was horrible. I tried to put up with Alex. I tried to reach out to the mom. Nothing. I got nothing back.

"This is my classroom. I'll make the rules," you vow. You spend the rest of the night planning how to resurrect your image and grab back control of your classroom.

In the morning you come to your senses. What does a vengeful approach do to improve the long-term version of your classroom?

You think through the punishment options and they all seem limited in addressing him acting out:

1. Isolate him by moving his seat away from other children.
2. Assign extra homework when he acts out in class.
3. Give him extra detentions until he is compliant.
4. Send him to the main office every time he acts out.
5. Single him out in front of the class.

Instead of just reacting, you decide to analyze each option.

Option 1. Isolate him by moving his seat away from other children. Although he is more distracted sitting next to his close friends in your class, he is so popular that it seems as if everyone is his friend. This would be a losing battle. You know that it would only be a matter of minutes before he pulled some other student off-task. This is a good start, but how does it address the core problem that he doesn't care about you or your classroom? The fundamental reality is that you don't have a connection with Alex. Isolating him will not improve his perspective on that reality.

Option 2. Assign extra homework when he acts out in class. Do you really want to assign more work to a student who is obviously behind academically? Yes, there is a slim possibility he might comply, but then what? Most likely, he will become resentful and even more vengeful. You can't force someone to like being in your room. And he doesn't see the value in being in your room.

Option 3. Give him extra detentions until he is compliant. Alex should be held accountable for wasting your time. But how well do detentions work anyway? In the short term—fantastic. As a die-hard policy—not so much. Alex may change. Will you serve the detentions with him? Do you have the time for that? Will you end up being a "bean counter" chalking up each of his infractions to document the need for a detention? What outlandish behavior will qualify as detention-worthy? How much more time will he steal from your other students while you fill in the paperwork to process and document his detentions?

Option 4. Send him to the main office every time he acts out. If you take this route, the power will reside with an administrator and not with you. You know he will be sent back to your class eventually. Instead, how do you make him want to be in your room?

Option 5. Single him out in front of the class. This is a very viable option. Alex cares deeply about his image. However, if you confront him in front of her peers, you are putting your fledgling reputation up against his well-developed social standing. This may work out for the class period, but a long-term fix is questionable at best. How would you fare in a test of wills with him? Is this really the role model you want to be? "I'm bigger than you and I'm an adult, therefore you have to do what I say." How will embarrassing him make him want to be in your room more?

What you really need is to use your social judo to pull him toward you instead of pushing him away.

→ WHAT IS YOUR NEXT MOVE?—P. 57

Option 5. Research Alex's School Records and Develop More Empathy

YOU enter the main office and ask one of the secretaries where the student cumulative files are. She looks up from her work, smiles at you, and directs you to the file cabinet.

Back in your credential program, you were told to do your research on each of your students—especially the ones who are monopolizing your time. You always intend to make this extra effort, but with so much going on in your life it seems as an overwhelming thing to start. Well, you are here now.

Watching the clock, you make a mental note of the time you start on this research. Within three minutes you have Alex's file in your hand. Man, is it thick. You don't know if this is a good thing or a bad thing. The file flops open on top on a side table. The first thing you see is his elementary school photo. He looked like a happy child. "What changed?" you mutter to yourself.

Looking at the photos, you notice subtle changes. Comparing the photos from fourth and fifth grades, you notice a slight slump in his shoulders and a new, creeping distant look in his eyes. You are intrigued. Time check—five minutes into this adventure.

What happened? It appears that there was a trigger event that spun Alex out of control. What was it? Is there anything you are doing in your instruction to fuel that fire? Time check—seven minutes.

There it is. Halfway through his fourth-grade year—well after the confident school picture was taken—his grades slumped, just like his shoulders eventually would in his fifth-grade picture.

The more you think about it, the reason could be any number of things: family split; economic downfall; catastrophic friend/social event; a disastrous teacher interaction (from his perspective, you may be the new disastrous interaction).

Empathy Break

You feel the heft of his folder. You think of the heft of his perspective of disappointment on his conscience.

So what do you do now? Should you coddle him? No way. No one likes to be babied. It is condescending. Should you ignore this new information? Impossible.

How about patience? That is feasible. Could you alter your view of him as a troubling/troubled time stealer? Probably. Could you talk with him in private and simply say, "I'm ready for a new start"? Easily. Would he ignore your outreach? Possibly. Does it matter if he ignores your outreach? Fundamentally, no, it doesn't. Time check—nine minutes.

You put his folder back in place in the file cabinet and thank the secretary for the help.

On the walk back to your classroom, you have one thought: You can't change Alex's past. You can affect his present in your classroom. What effect you have on his future will be determined by your generosity in his present.

➜ WHAT IS YOUR NEXT MOVE?—P. 57

Option 6. Change Your Pedagogical Approach

IT is a new day. You are standing outside of your classroom during the passing period, determined to truly see students. Alex appears. "Why does he keep coming back every day?" you ask yourself. Surely it isn't you. You are the teacher who makes him feel inadequate and lost. You stick out your hand to shake his, as you do for every student. He walks right past you. As you shake the next student's hand, you turn to see Alex come to life talking with one of his many friends in your room.

You think back to what you know about multiple learning styles. You decide that Alex is the prototypical interpersonal learner. What does an interpersonal learner need most? He needs to process out loud. That is why Alex is still talking about last Friday night on the following Wednesday. He needs processing time. He turns his back to you during your lectures, because you are not a reliable source for instruction in his eyes.

Empathy Break

You have been examining this entire experience through the wrong lens. Yes, it seems as though he is against you. But it isn't you as a person. Your instruction delivery system is falling short of his needs. This revelation depersonalizes this entire misadventure. Yet, you made it personal, because you have continued to ostracize him in your room.

You realize that you need to shift your focus so that you can appeal to an interpersonal learner. That will take new pedagogy. You need to use his strengths to guide his instruction. Instead of pushing against him to get your way, you need to pull him toward your content.

A quick review of your credential program notes helps you identify the answer: collaboration. When do you give students the opportunity to check in with their peers while you are presenting? This is a social skill you need to model and teach. You quickly revise your plan for tomorrow.

Today is a new day. You greet students as they enter your class. The warm-up review of yesterday's lesson is on the board. Alex ignores you as he walks in the room. You consciously model appropriate social interaction as you walk around the room during the warm-up time, talking with the students; checking for understanding; saying happy birthday to one girl; and essentially showing that you are human. After a quick review of the warm-up, you make the transition to whole-class instruction.

"I'm going to give you more time to check in with each other while I'm lecturing," you say. " Today, I'm going to model how I want you to talk with each other in my classroom." Your approach to assume nothing and be explicit in your expectations is brilliant. You feel this surge of confidence with every breath. Time check—two minutes into this adventure to shift your approach.

You turn to a student who has been working with you since the beginning of the school year. You are talking to the entire class as you stand near him. "Carlos, let's pretend both of us are students in this class. Let me rephrase that: I'll pretend to be a student; you pretend to be yourself." The class's chuckle gives you more confidence. Even Alex is now only pretending not to pay attention.

"So the teacher is lecturing and says something like, 'Please ask your partner if he or she has any questions about what I just said.' Carlos, please show me your absolutely worst behavior if you were given the opportunity to check in with another student. And I'll be the other student."

You sit down next to Carlos and put your feet on the desk. You move your shoulders away from Carlos and start yelling to a student across the room about last Friday night. Carlos is dumbfounded. Slowly, even he copies your actions. The class is dumbstruck. All they can do is laugh as you throw a wadded-up piece of paper toward the front of the room. Out of the corner of your eye, you see Alex crack his first smile of the year. Time check—four minutes. You stand up to indicate the simulation is over.

You then ask the class, "What was wrong with this? How would this behavior affect the class?" The class is more engaged than ever. Hands are shooting up left and right. You hear a cacophony of student voices:

> "No one can focus if everyone is doing that."

> "I wouldn't feel safe with stuff being thrown around."

> "My mom wants me to learn new stuff, not to play around."

And the insights go on and on . . .

"Carlos, let's do this right. So the teacher is lecturing and says something like, 'Please ask your partner if he or she has any questions about what I just said.' Carlos, show me your absolutely *best* behavior if you were given the opportunity to check in with another student. And I'll be the other student."

Both you and Carlos sit up in your chairs and move your desks so you face each other. You both maintain eye contact, as you say, "What did you hear the teacher say just now?"

Carlos responds, "Right now, we are supposed to be kind and listen to each other."

You stand up to indicate the simulation is over. You then ask the class, "What worked? How would this behavior affect the class?" Hands are shooting up left and right. You hear a cacophony of student voices:

> "I can live with that. You two seem to care about each other."

> "I would learn stuff."

> "My mom said I should act like that."

Time check—six minutes. You feel as though you have made real progress in modeling the behavior you want out of all students. Yes, Alex was your inspiration for change, but you quickly realize all students need reminders of how to work as a caring interactive classroom.

"Let's try this," you say. "From now on, I'll limit my instruction to five-minute blocks. I'll give you time to check in with each other, as long as you focus during my five minutes. Pinkie promise deal?"

Students chuckle as they hold up their pinkies and say in unison, "Pinkie promise."

By the end of class, you feel more confident than ever. You were able to get through the same amount of content, in the same amount of time. Classroom disruptions have disappeared. Students practiced talking with each other. As you circulated while students were talking, you had to redirect students on three occasions to talk about your subject content instead of YouTube videos. But all of this was manageable. All you had to say was, "Are you talking about what I just said?" It was your proximity that made the difference. You broke out of your comfort stage area. You are now working the entire room. You feel great.

→ WHAT IS YOUR NEXT MOVE?—P. 57

Option 7. Call in the Principal to Mediate

"So here we are," the principal says at the start of this closed door meeting with you and Alex's mom. "How did things spin so out of control? The probability of this working out in your favor seems further and further away. Fundamentally, you are in the customer service business. You provide an educational service, and your customer—the child and the parent—are not satisfied with your delivery. Clean-up time.

"I'm sure everyone here has done things they regret," the principal says, looking annoyed from behind her desk. She makes minimal eye contact with you. Her attention is appropriately focused on the client—the parent. "The goal of today's meeting is to create a solution together so Alex can thrive here on our campus. Why don't you start by telling me what happened?" The principal motions in the direction of Alex's mom.

"I don't know why you hired this person," the mother cries out, her words hitting you like pepper spray. "They doesn't teach. All they does is make my child feel as though he doesn't belong here." The mother goes on to describe your inefficiencies. Some of what she says is accurate. Some of what she says has been made up by Alex to help her case against you. You try to pay attention, but it is hard to focus.

After Alex's mom leaves, you get up to leave. "We need to talk," says the principal. "Now, we all mess up. And I have sat where you are sitting now. Heck, there isn't a week that goes by that a parent doesn't complain to me about something. Often they go directly to the district office. You won't please everyone all of the time, but this was something you could have controlled better.

"I have never met a parent who didn't want their child to do well. I have never met a child who didn't want to succeed. Most of the time, students don't know how to succeed. That is the difference between a teacher who is checking in and living for a paycheck and an educator who is actively trying to help mold young people to lead optimal lives. You have the makings of being an educator.

"Have you spoken with Mr. Gregor? I never have parent complaints about him. You could learn a lot from him. I highly suggest you reach out to Mr. Gregor."

→ WHAT IS YOUR NEXT MOVE?—P. 57

Option 8. Opt Out of Confrontation and Change Alex's Schedule with No Character Development Occurring

"What do I have to do to get Alex out of my class?" you mumble to the counselor. The school year is already more than a month old. Students' schedules are set. There is a balance of all of the other "Alexs" out there.

"Now what's happened?" The counselor asks calmly.

You look at the clock. You need to be back in your room in ten minutes. You still need to make copies for the afternoon, and who knows what you left written on your front white board. It is not the first time today that beads of sweat form at your temples.

"I don't know where to start. Maybe we should just reschedule this meeting. I need to go and get ready . . ."

"Stop and sit," says the counselor.

You sit. You take what feels like your first breath of the day. How did you end up appearing to be the bad guy? Alex is the menace. He is the one eating away at your time. He is the one who is preventing you from helping out all of the other students on your roster. If you could just avoid seeing him one more time, you could have some semblance of teacher normalcy . . .

You glance at your watch as you hear the counselor say again, "Breathe." Your class starts in five minutes. "Breathe. Now tell me what happened."

It really only takes five minutes to dissect all of your past failings with Alex. On hearing your own voice, you realize it isn't that bad. Alex can be a menace. He is disruptive. He is rude. He is vindictive.

"What do you think your classroom is like from Alex's point of view?" the counselor asks. She is no longer sitting behind the desk. She is now sitting across from you. You lean back in your chair. Breathe. Breathe. Breathe.

"What is my classroom like from Alex's point of view?" You have never considered this before. Yes, you teach kindness, social responsibility and all of that "whole child" stuff. "What *is* my classroom like from Alex's point of view?"

Breathe. Breathe. Breathe. You hear the counselor's voice in your head the rest of the afternoon, alternating with your attempts at answering that important question: What is my classroom like from Alex's point of view?

→ WHAT IS YOUR NEXT MOVE?—P. 57

Option 9. Reach Out to a Trusted Colleague for Suggestions, Promoting Collegiality

IT is first thing in the morning. You turn around and see one of your colleagues walking toward you. No students have arrived on campus yet. Why is this guy always so "up"?

"Nice to see you today," he greets you.

"Hey," you grumble. Why is your colleague always so optimistic? Doesn't he know he will be overrun with students in a few minutes, just like you and every other adult on campus?

Empathy Break

You realize this teacher loves his job. What is his secret? You both teach the same content. You are hard-pressed to think of a time he shared your beaten-down body posture. His shoulders are back; his head is up. He seems excited to start his day. He *always* seems excited to start his day. What is his secret?

It suddenly occurs to you that his positive attitude might be helpful to you in your problem with Alex. "Can I talk with you for a second?" you mumble as you turn and face him. "Sure. What's going on?" Your colleague seems genuinely interested.

You tell him the whole sad story of Alex. He doesn't interrupt. He maintains eye contact throughout. There isn't any head shaking. You don't feel judged as you talk in detail about your ordeal. It feels as though you have been talking for hours, because you feel tired just retelling your limited success and overwhelming failure with this child. In reality, only four minutes have passed.

"Wow. That sounds rough." He seems to genuinely share your grief. "What can I do to make your life easier?"

You weren't expecting this response. You just wanted to unload. "I don't know. What do you have in mind?" You stammer.

"How about we meet after school for twenty minutes? I have some simple quick fixes for you. But to make any significant change in your year, we really need to talk. Do you mind if I swing by during my preparatory period for ten minutes so I can get a feeling for how you run your classroom? I'll take some notes so we have some talking points. I'm on your side. Maybe you can spend ten minutes observing in my classroom as well. My classroom is never perfect. I'm always interested in another set of eyes and feedback on how I can improve what I do. When can you stop by?"

Oh no. Not another thing to do. Doesn't he realize you already have a mammoth stack of papers you are behind on? Your preparatory period is already filled with lesson planning.

"Sure, I'm in." Your shoulders roll back slightly as you make a commitment toward collaboration. You feel the same sense of confidence you once felt a long time ago before the Alex disaster.

"Great. I'll see you later today," your colleague says as he walks away. You look down at your watch. Time check—five minutes. Change really doesn't take as long as you thought. This might be doable.

Throughout the day, you are focused on your instruction but your mind drifts to your afternoon meeting. What could a quick fix look like? What does the big picture look like?

Later in the day, you are nervous when you see him walk in to your room during your instruction. You feel under the microscope as you would with any observer. Your colleague quietly sits in the back of your room. His facial expression doesn't change during his ten minutes there. He is taking notes as he said he would. What is he seeing that you aren't?

During your prep, you stop by his classroom. Controlled chaos is the best description for it. Students are up out of their seats, collaborating, talking respectfully to each other. In ten minutes, your colleague asked for their attention on two different occasions to clarify instructions. He didn't need to raise his voice. All he did was ask for their attention, and all students became quiet within five seconds. When he was finished "checking in," as he called it, students immediately resumed their work. The best descriptors that come to mind are engaged, dynamic, focused, social, and fun. School could be fun? How did he pull this off?

By 3 p.m. you are definitely intrigued. Your colleague greets with you a smile. "My time is yours until 3:30. I need to be home by 4 p.m. when my child care ends for the day." You realize that you can't remember when your colleague didn't make time to help someone, but he always sets time limits. Maybe this is why he always seems so calm.

"What did you see in my room?" you ask. "Your classroom seemed so fluid. How did you pull that off? I wasn't there for very long, but I didn't see you reprimand a single student. What is your secret?"

"Nothing is a secret. We are in the people business. What do you know about your students?"

You are startled by his question. Where to start? "I know my special education students. I know how they performed on last year's state test. I also know, ummm . . . "

"We all know those things," he cuts you off. "Maybe I wasn't clear. How well do you know your students? We are all more than just assigned numbers from a test score or special needs placement. I know we all have a massive class load, but I call every home at the beginning of the school year.

"On the first day of school, my students fill in a personal inventory sheet (p. 67). I then spend roughly ten hours total during the first week and weekend, calling each one of my students' parents. I start each phone call in the same way: 'Hi, I'm your child's new teacher. From my experience, the better connection we have between your home and my classroom, the more each child will thrive. What would you like for me to know about your child so he can thrive this school year?' And then I listen and take notes. While I'm listening, I try to memorize each child's personal histories. To work well with a child, you need to get to know the whole person. This makes allies out of parents. You model the empathy you want students to model to each other. Nothing is perfect, but the simple gesture of calling home gives me an 'in' with students. I think this is one of the main things I do to cut down disruptions in my classroom."

You are skeptical. You know there is more going on than a simple investment of ten hours. Your mind starts to do the quick math for the school year—185 days. If each class period is forty-five minutes on average, each teacher invests roughly 120 hours on each student during the school year. (This is obviously minus minimum days, fire drills, assemblies, and other distractions.) This works out to 7,200 minutes of instruction per class period. If each phone call takes five minutes that cost benefit analysis is a good investment, which means the student benefits and the families benefit. Ultimately, you benefit by laying down the environment for you to be a teacher instead of a drill sergeant.

"What are quick fixes?" Your interest is completely piqued.

"Meet students at the door. A presence in the hallways is huge. Be social. Joke around with them. Be you. Measure them up before they come into your room. If a child's shoulders are drooping—I know a lot of students slouch—but really look at the shoulders. Focus on body posture. Shoulders tell you everything. If a student is walking with her shoulders back and looking up, that is a sure sign she is confident. Hunched shoulders means defeated and tired. If a student is walking with one shoulder higher than the other, slanted looking, he is confused.

"Also, read eyes. A distracted look tells you something is going on. Pull students aside before they enter. Ask them how they are. Once you can convince a student you care, why should she ever act out in your room to get back at you? If you have a connection with a student; if you can convince her that you care; when she acts out, it is a telegraphed message for help. To teach the whole child, a teacher should have academic as well as personal goals for each student. Personal goals should include: kindness, generosity, empathy, graciousness to name just a few lofty characteristics," your colleague says.

Time check—five minutes. "You remind me of a teacher during my credential program" you say. "She always said, 'You get what you give.' I'm so tired and burnt out. I don't have the time for these 'extras.'"

"Think about the time you are spending now," he responds. "How much of your day is spent cleaning up earlier messes instead of being proactive and reaching out first?"

"What are some other fixes?"

"Never talk over students. Take a long pause. If a student is engaged in a private conversation, there is no way he can hear your instructions. Praise in public and correct in private. Once again you are modeling the person you want students to be. What I always tell students is, 'Your ability to focus determines everything in your life. Therefore, when you are talking, I stop and focus on your needs.' You'll be amazed how responsive students are when they feel respected. If a student is starting to take advantage of you, walk over to her and camp out. Look at the child and wait for attention. The less you say the more power you have.

"With all of that said, students need limits. The only way for students to grow and thrive is within boundaries. It is the job of each of us to help give honest feedback to students. If Alex is acting out, don't be afraid to send him to the main office. He should have consequences for his actions. But always think: how can you provide an environment where he doesn't need to act out. To get there, you need to know your students and differentiate your teaching."

"What do you mean by differentiating?" You are hitting information overload.

"I can see that you are burnt. We'll talk again soon."

Time check—ten minutes. *Are you going to adopt what this veteran teacher says?*

➜ WHAT IS YOUR NEXT MOVE?—P. 57

Student Information Sheet

Name: _____ Home Phone: (____) _____-_____
　　　　　Last　　　　First　　　　Middle

Address:_____
　　　　　　Number　　　　Street　　　　City　　　　Zip Code

Birthday: _____ Birthplace: _____
　　　　Month　Day　Year　　　　　　　　　City　　　　　Country

Name of the adults with whom you live:　　Relationship to you:　　Daytime Phone:

　　　　　　　　　　　　　　　　　　　　　　　　　　　　　　　(____) _____-_____
_____　_____
　　Last　　　　First

　　　　　　　　　　　　　　　　　　　　　　　　　　　　　　　(____) _____-_____
_____　_____
　　Last　　　　First

　　　　　　　　　　　　　　　　　　　　　　　　　　　　　　　(____) _____-_____
_____　_____
　　Last　　　　First

Names and ages of brothers and sisters with whom you live: _____

_____

_____

Name something(s) you do at school that you feel you are good at: _____

_____

_____

Name something(s) you do outside of school that you feel you are good at: _____

_____

_____

Favorite thing you did this summer: _____

_____

_____

Language arts teacher last year: _____

Social studies teacher last year: _____

Who is the most important person in your life? _____

_____

_____

What language do you speak most of the time at home? _____

_____

What other languages you can speak? _____

_____

What is the name of an adult member of your household who speaks and reads English? _____

_____

Do you usually ride the bus to and from school?   Yes   No

Do you usually help take care of younger siblings at home?   Yes   No

What is the most important thing for us to know about you? _____

_____

_____

Is there anything else you would like us to know about you? _____

_____

_____

List your class schedule in the space below:

Period	Teacher	Room	Subject
1st	_____	_____	_____
2nd	_____	_____	_____
3rd	_____	_____	_____
4th	_____	_____	_____
5th	_____	_____	_____
6th	_____	_____	_____
7th	_____	_____	_____

Who are your heroes? Why? What qualities do they have that you respect? _____

_____

_____

_____

What pets do you have and what are their names? _____

_____

_____

List five things you can't live without: _____

_____

_____

_____

Title of the last book you read and enjoyed: _____

_____

Best movie you have seen: _____

_____

I have an account on the following social networking sites (circle all that apply):

     MySpace   Xanga   Facebook   Instagram   Twitter   Other

Are your profiles private? They *should* be!

If you could be anywhere in the world right now, where would you be and why? _____

_____

_____

Describe your ideal life when you are 25 years old: _____

_____

_____

_____

_____

_____

What are five of your goals for this school year? _____

_____

_____

What bothers you the most at school? _____

_____

_____

When you grow up, what would you like to do as a profession? Why? _____

_____

_____

Student Name: _____

Parent Conference Documentation

Date	Person Contacted	Notes
_____	_____	_____
_____	_____	_____
_____	_____	_____
_____	_____	_____

7. Giving Praise to Individuals or to the Entire Class

THE classroom is humming. Students are energetic walking in the classroom. Your assignment on-time turn-in rate is higher than 90 percent. Classroom disruptions are few and far between. You are starting to feel as though you have a handle on this new teaching adventure. However, teaching is just like every other aspect of life. The moment you get comfortable, you start to lose ground. The metaphor of rowing against the tide comes to mind. Unless you are diligent and keep up your effort, you quickly fall back to where you started.

One night you decide to do some research about job satisfaction. According to a Gallup Research study of more than 4 million workers worldwide:

- The number-one reason people leave their jobs: They don't feel appreciated.
- 65% of Americans received no recognition in the workplace in the year of the study (2011).
- Of those surveyed, 9 out of 10 said they were *more* productive when they worked around positive people (Rath and Clifton 2009).

School is our children's work world. So here is your challenge. How do you keep the good vibe flowing so students can thrive, feel genuinely appreciated, and want to embrace challenges that become larger and more complicated every day?

How much class time can you sacrifice to feel-good moments to build student morale? What happens if you do nothing? You have so much instructional material to cover, how could you possibly devote time to praise? And why do students need to be praised for doing what they should be doing already?

You have a lot of questions to consider as you tinker with your program to keep things positive in your classroom.

So what is your next move? You:

1. Throw a pizza party—p. 74
2. Implement Fred Jones's Preferred Activity Time—p. 76
3. Set expectations through the use of contracts—p. 77
4. Develop and maintain a monthly incentive program—p. 79
5. Change rewards so all students can win—p. 82
6. Become Mr. or Ms. DVD—p. 83
7. Maintain the day-to-day grind of keeping things positive in your classroom—p. 83

Following is a discussion of each option. You can move to from one to the next, or you can jump between options at any time.

Option 1. Throw a Pizza Party

WHAT a great class you have this year! You heard other teachers using pizza parties as a reward, and you thought it would be fun. This is a terrific option if the following criteria apply to your situation:

1. The entire class has earned it. If you have a noncompliant student, you will have to make special accommodations for that student while other students' success is celebrated.
2. You have the means to maintain this level of incentive. Can you afford to pay for multiple pizza parties during the year?
3. You can justify throwing a pizza party and still not fall behind schedule in pursuing student proficiency in academic standards.

When you ask other teachers, the ones who use pizza parties as incentives seem to have wonderful classroom management. Don't be fooled. The most effective teachers use pizza parties as rewards but not to drive their classroom management. Embedding incentives throughout your academic year is essential, but any teacher needs to be aware of how incentives are perceived.

As you recognize student achievement, you refer back to your teacher training notes to look up "locus of control." You read: "The extent to which people believe they have power over events in their lives. A person with an internal locus of control believes that he or she can influence events and their outcomes, while someone with an external locus of control blames outside forces for everything."

This concept was brought to light in the 1950s by Julian Rotter. The underlying question regarding the locus of control is this . . . do I control my life or does something else (like a God or fate) control it? This simple idea has profound significance as it influences peoples' beliefs very strongly. Do you believe in God? Are you an agnostic? Why? Do I just have good luck? If I make all the right decisions does that mean I can make my life be exactly how I envision it? These are all questions that might arise from that simple premise" (Fournier 2009).

The inherent goal of any effective academic program is to nurture individual competency and responsibility in accordance with high standards. In other words, your ultimate teaching goal is to nurture internal locus of control whereby your students develop into people who are in control of their own destiny. If students perceive that their work was the causal agent in creating the opportunity to have a pizza party, then your goals are starting to be met. If students are not aware of the causal relationship, then any pizza party runs counter to your year-long goals.

The more you think about it, the more you realize that, as with everything in your teaching career, an effective educator needs to be clear in the purpose of the work, frank in the delivery of the information, and continually check for understanding—even with a pizza party.

Now that a pizza party seems like a solid possibility, you take on the implementation issues:

Consideration 1: Who has earned it? First, you must decide what you are rewarding with the party. Are you rewarding students who collect the most cans for a food drive? That is unacceptable, socially and ethically. However, if your students have been working well and have been compliant, a pizza party may be an appropriate reward.

So has the entire class earned the party, or do you have a few noncompliant students (like most teachers do) who have not earned it? You will have to make special accommodations for them, and those accommodations should always center on maintaining high expectations and giving a student a way out.

Consideration 2: Maintaining the incentive. Once you start any incentive program like a pizza party, your students will expect you to follow through with this multiple times during the year.

For a select few teachers, money is not an issue. For a majority of teachers, money *is* an issue. When you think about asking parents to contribute for a pizza party, you wonder: Does the pizza party lose its authenticity if parents pay for it? What will you do with the contribution of the parents of a noncompliant student who will not be invited to the celebration? How will you ease any social issues that will arise from families who can't or don't want to contribute? How much time do you have to keep track of all of this? You find that collecting money for any incentive can spin out of control. You will need to have superior organizational skills throughout the process. All in all, collecting money from families for a pizza party is a net loss in any cost/benefit analysis.

Consideration 3: Do you have the time? To keep from using class time for this party, your best option is to hold it in your classroom at lunch. This has the potential to unify students. They will love to be with each other, hang out, and just enjoy the moment.

Once you have addressed the three considerations of who will attend, how you will sustain your incentive plan, and making time for it, there are seven steps to pulling off the party.

Step 1. Make sure you have administrative support. You decide to tell your administration your intent to have a pizza party; how you plan on paying for it; why it is necessary; and how you will limit the impact on the custodial staff.

Step 2. Make sure the food will arrive on time. Order the day before, so if there are any emergencies on the day of the party, you are not frantically trying to order pizzas and teach at the same time.

Step 3. Take care of any students who have dietary restrictions. If you are the host of the party, you need to make sure your guests feel welcome.

Step 4. Keep stragglers out. Once word gets out that you are throwing a pizza party, students you have never seen may show up at your door or take a seat in the front of your room.

Step 5. Link the pizza as a meaningful reward for students adhering to your academic and behavioral expectations. Before you pass out the pizza, do you have a reflection moment? Do you say a few words? Best yet, do you have a student say a few words connecting the celebration with the class's actions, which made the moment possible?

Step 6. Pass out the pizza in a quick and equitable way. Students should take two smaller pieces first and have seconds later, if there is enough pizza left.

Step 7. Hold students accountable to clean up. What is the inherent behavioral message you will be giving students if they eat and then leave all of the work to you, the host teacher?

So, is this pizza party enough?

→ WHAT IS YOUR NEXT MOVE?—P. 73

Option 2. Implement Fred Jones's Preferred Activity Time[1]

FRED Jones's work to support positive classroom management and positive classroom instruction is unmatched. After reading his must-have book, *Tools for Teaching* (2007), you decide to implement Preferred Activity Time (PAT) in your classroom. This section is a summation of Fred Jones's work.

Just like your instruction, the ultimate goal of PAT is to guide students to independence according to exemplary academic and social standards. Under this umbrella are explicit teaching practices and social accountability. First and foremost, you have already set up your classroom to enable PAT to work. You want to catch students doing things right, but you also need to maintain a physical presence to reinforce your behavioral standards. You have the students' desks in your room set up so you can reach any student within four strides. The scene is set so you can manage your classroom with close conversations to redirect off-task students back on track.

Setting up your classroom: In the front of your room you have set up a T-chart scorecard with a positive sign on one side and a negative sign on the other. This T-chart is no larger than it needs to be to be seen throughout the classroom. You have used electrical tape to form the T. You know you will need a different T-chart for each class of students you teach, so you use different-colored electrical tape for each class. Your ultimate goal is to ditch this T-chart as soon as your students earn it—ideally at the start of the second semester.

Implementing PAT: During your introduction of PAT, your priority is to plant the seeds of optimism and a team spirit: "Today we will start Preferred Activity Time, otherwise known as PAT. My goal is give back to you the class time you save. When everyone is here on time, I'll mark the time you save on this T-chart. Just for hearing me out right now, I'll put ten minutes into your class's time bank. When I see you helping out another student at an appropriate time, I'll mark more time in. Best yet, because my goal is for you to own your education, quite often I'll toss you a marker and ask you to put up a few minutes. I want to catch you doing things right. So that we have the same expectations, what are some examples of actions you can take to show me you are being responsible for your education?"

Without commenting, you notate the student-generated list of positive student behaviors right next to the PAT score sheet. Because it is early in the school year, your students still want to make a positive first impression. Therefore, the vast majority of comments will be in the reasonable range. It is in your best interest to ignore any outlier, attention-seeking, ridiculous comment. You decide to not lose focus on modeling the positive behavior you want your students to adhere to. This subtle move of a student-generated list of ways to help the class generates more student buy-in, because the students have a direct say in how the program will be measured.

"This is a fantastic start, and I agree to your list," you say. "Many of you have already seen the negative side of the list. I'm sure you have already figured this out. Yes, I will also be marking down time lost. One of the main ideas from my classroom is the importance of thinking beyond yourself. Your actions affect the rest of our class. When you make the choice to be off-task, it is more difficult for our class to meet our goals. It will be a rare occurrence for me to mark any negative time, because I'm sure you will rise to the expectation of the class.

---

1 The value of Fred Jones's work to any teacher cannot be overemphasized. Attending a Fred Jones workshop could easily be the best move any teacher might make in terms of professional development.

"Naturally, you're thinking, 'So what are all of these marks for? On Review Day Thursday, you will have the privilege of cashing in your PAT for review games before Friday's test. Games will vary from Jeopardy, to Charades, to Pictionary, to Who Wants to be a Social Studies Genius?, and so on. The key to this program is that you earn it. So let's get to work."

Within the first five minutes of your instruction, you need to walk the walk. You catch a student on task and you note some minutes. You circulate during your instruction. You have students check in with each other. Within reason, you acknowledge your students who are buying into your program and saving you time. You know that you don't want to give away the entire store to earn a few customers, but during the first few weeks of this program, you add points every day to maintain hope.

On Wednesday, you have a student count the points accrued. Students have earned only fifteen minutes of PAT, so you spend only fifteen minutes playing the review game. You find that it is easy to lose perspective of your overall goals when you start up a new program. Your goal is to address your learning goals for students. With this focus in mind, you know that PAT should never be cashed in for "hanging out" time or other non-academic events. You must maintain the integrity of what you do.

So now you have put in the essential Fred Jones elements to keep your good vibe going.

A student decides to waste your instructional time, and you try to keep in mind to praise in public and correct in private. You walk over to the child's desk and "camp out." You put your hands on the desk and wait. Twenty seconds seems like an eternity, but it really is only twenty seconds. You wait for the students' attention. Before you go, you whisper, "Are you confused about what I am expecting from you right now? No? We are on problem five. I know you can do better." And then you leave to continue your work teaching the class content. On the T-chart, you note the time lost.

Most likely, you will have an attention glutton who will continue to act out because he or she thinks that that is the best way to get your undivided attention. Your best bet is to not add fuel to the fire. Fred Jones calls this "omission training." If the attention glutton student acts out, he or she can no longer play the role of the villain and take away points. He or she can only add points. Make the student the hero. Give bonus points for times when the student does something great.

➜ WHAT IS YOUR NEXT MOVE?—P. 73

Option 3. Set Expectations Through the Use of Contracts

EFFECTIVE praise comes from setting limits. There is nothing wrong with being strict with a student if he or she violates a limit. Students want to be held accountable. The collateral for building relationships with students is to catch them doing things right and praise them for it in public.

How do you set limits? Initially, your conversations with a student who has violated a limit need to be behavior-focused and not personal. What is important here is giving the student a way out—a way to leave the conversation feeling more optimistic and hopeful. You must pull back from frustration with your noncompliant student and look at the big picture. She has a long life ahead of her. Your job is to nurture and model second chances. That is why you are effectively responding to her actions by setting more specific limits. She needs an academic/behavior contract and she needs you to respect her enough to be honest. (See the sample contract at the end of this chapter).

When you present the contract to one student, your private conversation goes like this:

"I want to be very clear about what we are talking about," you say. "You are not living up to your potential. Often students and adults alike get confused between personhood and actions. You as a person—fantastic. I've seen you act graciously and with compassion with your classmates.

Important Note

This part of the conversation is just as important to you as it is to the student. A professional teacher's goal is to see the good in everyone. Go into the conversation knowing this student. Develop your empathy for him or her. This child is acting out ultimately because he or she is not comfortable with the environment. By being a positive influence, you do your part to make that student more comfortable in your classroom.

"You as a person are highly valued in our classroom community. You and I both know you are not participating in today's invitation-only event because you need to improve your work ethic and social awareness.

Important Note

Opening up your monologue to a dialogue can be tricky. Ask, "What do you think?" only if you are ready to hear the response. Most likely, the child sees you in a negative light. The last thing you want is for this child to slide into a full-fledged argument. You will never come out the winner. If the child interrupts you, simply walk away. If the child follows you, hurling insults along the way, *do not engage*. Instead, fill in a referral notice and send the child with an escort (your most trusted student) to the principal.

"Specifically, you have not completed these assignments to your fullest potential." You then list the assignments this student has not turned in.

Last week, you had this conversation with a student whose issue was, instead, behavioral. You said many of the same things to her, until you came to the reason for the conversation: "Based on your actions," you said, "you have not earned the privilege to join our invitation-only event today." You then outlined the specific behaviors that were getting in the student's way. You closed that conversation and are closing this one with the presentation of the contract.

"I'm going to give you a way out. I have developed this Behavior and Academic Contract, which I would like you to sign. This is where you can have a direct say in how you want me to acknowledge your success and help you turn around your year. I want you to earn an opportunity to participate in this event." You ask that the student look over the contract and finish the outstanding assignment.

You asked last week's student to write an authentic apology letter to atone for the wrongful behavior.

"I will come back to check your work," you finish up, "and I will gladly welcome you to join the rest of the class. Until then, please sit in this desk facing the wall, and get to work. I'm confident you will earn our next invitation-only event."

Important Note

If you have multiple students who have not earned this incentive, it is up to you to read the scene. Your top priority is to get back to the students who are doing well. Don't lose yourself in a confrontation with your noncompliant students. You may want to conduct two conversations—one with the academically ineligible students and another with the behaviorally ineligible students. While you are talking with one group, have the other group look over the Behavior and Academic Contract. Or talk with all of your non-invitees at once. Make sure their workspaces are separated. During your invitation-only event, you will need to check on these students' progress.

It is important to consider your own potential biases. Are there any trends, in terms of race or gender, in the students who do not earn your events? When you look around the room, veer away from blaming the victim. You are the adult in the room and you should be acting like it—always. Invitation-only events are wonderful moments for you to look at your successes and your shortcomings. The students who are not earning your events are those that you are not serving well enough. No one is perfect, but your unending job is to continue to strive for perfection, inclusion, and student success.

→ WHAT IS YOUR NEXT MOVE?—P. 73

Option 4. Develop and Maintain a Monthly Incentive Program

As you planned your year, you made room in your calendar for monthly incentives for students. At Back-to-School Night, you talked to parents about giving students those monthly incentives. Now is the time for you to implement your plan.

An invitation-only event is a culminating one-day lesson whereby students apply the content they learned in your classroom. *The invitation-only element is critical.* Students need to do the actual work to earn the privilege of participating in this event. Standards-reinforcing, unit-culminating monthly incentive events are essential for multiple reasons:

First, culminating invitation-only events, in which students can demonstrate their mastery, give students classroom goals. Your students will move beyond simply marching through the textbook. With incentive events, students have creative outlets to demonstrate their understanding of the material in new and unique out-of-the-textbook ways. Remember, though, to use these events sparingly—no more than once a month—or you will water down their importance to students. In addition, you need to be firm about expecting students to earn these privileges. The moment you give students an unearned benefit, you devalue those benefits.

Second, as students collect their invitations to these events throughout the year, you can work together track their success. You will be amazed by how many students will hold on to their invitations throughout the year so they can chronicle their achievements.

Last, these events reinforce standards. All of your end-of-the-unit invitation events must be standards-based to maintain the academic integrity your classroom deserves. You have some ideas for invitation-only events for your class. Many offer opportunities for including parents:[2]

September, Sidewalk Chalk: You can hold your first event outdoors, and this particular event allows you to incorporate art, an important component for students. Students can use sidewalk chalk to demonstrate their understanding of a plot diagram, sentence structure, symbolism, affixes, or vocabulary, among other concepts. To respect your neighbors, confine the space they will be working in and warn other teachers of the upcoming event.

October, Indoor Campfire: In the weeks before Halloween, students can write suspenseful scary stories. Then students can read aloud their stories, or retell famous stories, with the lights off and just a flashlight under their faces. On your class projector, you can show an actual campfire in the background. S'mores would complete the experience.

November, Thanksgiving Multicultural Feast:[3] In preparation for the feast, students will research their family's history and write a report, including a short piece on the person who has inspired them the most in their lives. This highlights interviewing skills, community inclusion, and personalization in one lesson. The final report's focus is on family pride, resiliency, and migration patterns over the past 150 years. To earn the privilege of participating in the feast, students give an oral presentation of their written reports. Students will take notes on each other's presentations. For a final exam, students can transform their notes to a time line of the past 150 years, showing which world events affected the personal histories of the students in the classroom. The student-created time lines provide a starting point for understanding the literature that will be covered for the rest of the school year. For the actual incentive, students can bring in a home-cooked dish to share with the rest of the class.

December, Beat Café and Poetry Slam: Students will analyze, create, and share poetry for several weeks. Applying poetry terms adds weight to literature analyses of poems. Each day's lesson can highlight a different type of poetry. Referring back to the newly created family history time lines solidifies students' understanding of the historical events that influenced each author's writing. Students who create their own poetry books (which doubles as a terrific holiday present) will be invited to two end-of- unit, invitation-only events—Beat Café and Poetry Slam. Across two days, students can experience firsthand how poetry readings have evolved over time. Decked out in sunglasses and berets and sipping hot cocoa, students will read their own poetry out loud. The next day students will engage in a 1980s Poetry Slam with microphones, backbeats, screaming fans, and judges.

January, No Name Calling Week Skits: So far in the school year, students will have developed different writing skills: summaries (September and October), narratives (October and November), research (November), and literature analysis (October and December). To prepare for No Name Calling Week, students will work on their persuasive writing skills by tackling bullying. *The Misfits* by James Howe has been the inspiration

---

2 These events, as presented here, would be appropriate for a seventh-grade class. You can adjust the parameters up or down for your students' grade level and skills.

3 The ideas for November, December, and May were adapted from the work of Eric Kruger. (See footnote, page 120)..

behind two national movements—Mix-It-Up Day and No Name Calling Week. After reading this very approachable text, students will write two more assignments—a research-based anti-bullying persuasive paper and a script of how to stand one's ground when faced with a bully. To help reinforce students' skills in advocating for themselves, they need guided practice. Writing, directing, and performing skits modeled after real-life bullying moments will empower all of your students to not be victims. Performing these skits in front of sixth graders elevates this invitation-only event to service learning and enables you to put into practice an ideal of teaching advocacy.

February, *The Outsiders* Movie Day: By now, students will have learned the value of invitation-only events, so there will be nothing wrong with showing a relevant movie. After spending multiple weeks reading S. E. Hinton's masterpiece, *The Outsiders,* students who finished the work for the book can see the movie. Students can take Cornell notes during the movie, comparing how themes they saw in the book are represented in the movie. This will be an ideal work time for you to tutor one on one with the students who struggled to finish analyzing the book.

March, Game Day for State Test Preparation: Traditionally, more than two-thirds of state tests focus on informational text. Giving students the opportunity to design their own board game and write the directions of playing will actually reinforce understanding of informational text. Students will love diagramming their board and elaborating on the elements of play. Spending a game day gives students an opportunity to practice reading informational text created by their fellow students.

April, College Field Trip: After reading John Steinbeck's *The Pearl,* students will see firsthand the effects a dystopian racist society can have on its inhabitants. Tying in Joseph Campbell's "hero's journey" outline (1968) will enable students to see that self-doubt is usually the greatest barrier to success. Education and controlling one's own destiny are major themes of Steinbeck's work. Arranging a field trip to a local college can bridge the values of a novel to your students' real lives.

May, Utopia Creation: Students can end the year creating their own ideal society. Developing a working vision of how they want their world to work gives them full proprietorship of their life paths.

June, City Council Forum: Is there a better way to empower students to develop the art of persuasion than by talking with local elected leaders about their Utopian visions? You can invite a local official to chat with students.

Culminating events can always be cross-curricular. You will look for ways to tie in Art, Drama, Foreign language, Math, Music, P.E., and Social Studies curricula to your events.

As you plan your first event, you start work on your invitation template. Each will be a half sheet of paper, so you can create two on a single piece of 8 ½" x 11" paper and then copy that one before cutting all of the pages in half. You give the invitation a banner heading: "Congratulations! You earned _____" or "You're Invited!"

Students love to publically praise other students, because they know they will have their own time in the sun soon. Little things advance that kind, inclusive mind-set. Have other students transcribe the class list of student names on these half sheets the week before you will pass out invitations. Holding on to the invitations of those students who did not earn them helps you document your case to a disgruntled parent.

Now, what do you do with the "stay-behinds," students who are not sold on producing work to demonstrate academic competency? They can use this class time to work on missing assignments. You may need to coordinate with a colleague to swap students for each other's culminating events.

And what do you do if the same students are consistently missing out on these events? You will first need to determine if a particular student's issue is cognitive. If so, then you will need to make accommodations. If the issue is, instead, a lack of motivation, you need to stay consistent on who is allowed to participate in the events. Those who are not motivated should not earn the rewards of the students who are.

You realize that the first few times you do this, you may have a lot of students who are noncompliant. This number will dwindle as the year progresses and students see that you cannot be bribed and whining doesn't win.

➜ WHAT IS YOUR NEXT MOVE?—P. 73

Option 5. Change Rewards So All Students Can Win

YOU will see many inspirational posters during your career. One of those is titled "101 Ways to Praise a Child." All of these pithy comments rely on personalization to have any authenticity. In the same vein, your incentives need to be pertinent to have any merit with students, so the first step is to know your students' needs. In any incentive program, you know you need to communicate what is coming, check comprehension of the concept during instruction, and clarify understanding after the instruction. Your incentive program will follow that format:

Step 1. Communicate the upcoming incentive and sell it: For students to care and work toward the incentive, you need to sell its importance. The more exciting you make your incentive, the more students will want to work to earn it. You need to know what is cool for your age group and twist it so it reinforces the academic standards you need to teach. If the goal is for students to demonstrate mastery of the standards and own their educational process, an outstanding option is for them to generate their own incentive event.

Step 2. Check for adherence to the incentive: You need to be clear about the prerequisites to earn an incentive, including what behavior you expect. Because your classroom runs on courtesy, you should have few, if any, behavior problems during an event. In addition, you will need an exit plan for noncompliant students. Your focus should never sway from reinforcing the connection between your class's hard work and the incentive.

Step 3. Bring closure to the incentive: You need to make sure the meaning behind your incentive is clear. Your top priority is to teach the standards. You decided a long time ago that you didn't need to be your students' friend. For you to maintain your diligence regarding standards, your invitation-only events must be unwaveringly standards-based.

➜ WHAT IS YOUR NEXT MOVE?—P. 73

Option 6. Become Mr. or Ms. DVD

THESE colleagues are experts on hitting "play" on the VCR or DVD. However, there is nothing wrong with using as many tools as you can to diversify your pedagogy. Movie days are simply another way for students to explore content on some days and be rewarded for diligent work on others. As with everything in life, balance is the key. With this in mind, as you look around campus, you see your school's "Ms. DVD." You hear the sound of another movie emanating from her subdued classroom. You think to yourself, "Really? Another movie?"

Then you remind yourself that you never know what other people might be going through. However, when you consider her reliance on DVDs, you have a difficult time not seeing the constant use of movies as professional negligence. Is her teaching message to plug in and play or interact? By not interacting with students, how is she going to develop any depth of understanding or depth of connection?

You find that you have some questions. How often should you reward students with a movie day? You believe that a movie every week is overboard and negligent. Teaching is just like cooking; too much of any one ingredient can kill any meal.

How will a movie affect attendance? If students know you as Mr. or Ms. Movie Friday, you should anticipate an increase in truancy.

What effect would showing movies have on your curriculum? As with everything you do, are you teaching to the academic standards and personalizing your instruction to multiple learning modalities?

Before you commit to movies as rewards, analyze your year. Pull back and examine the cadence of your year. Movie rewards are great if they reinforce your academic standards and personalize your instruction. Used more than necessary would just fill time for your students. As in life, balance is the key.

➜ WHAT IS YOUR NEXT MOVE?—P. 73

Option 7. Maintain the Day-to-Day Grind of Keeping Things Positive in Your Classroom

THE ultimate importance of a positive classroom is that it will be an environment in which students feel known, appreciated, and motivated to stretch themselves beyond what they thought was possible. You break down how each component of a positive environment is demonstrated in your classroom:

Ways in Which Students Feel Known:

1. You compliment students in genuine ways. Too many students spend an entire day, month, or year being wallpaper at school. Always there, but never noticed. The effort you invest in noticing a haircut or new braces goes a huge way to help a wallpaper student overcome his or her own social anxiety.
2. You open up and tell your class what type of student you were at their age. In this way, you model courage and make connections with students.

3. Students sign up to take turns—one each day—telling an appropriate joke or story. If a student is stuck, you make a stack of conversation starters available. This standards-reinforcing five-minute daily class opener is invaluable in so many ways. Students overcome presentation anxiety. Audience membership skills are reinforced. If a student is absent on his or her presentation day, you have two presenters the next day. In this way, students make themselves known in your classroom.

Making the subtle connections, convincing, reinforcing, and maintaining an interest in your students' lives, is immeasurable in keeping things positive.

Ways in Which Students Feel Appreciated:

1. You celebrate students' birthdays. At the beginning of the school year, you devote fifteen minutes to writing down each student's birthday on a calendar. Before the first birthday, you go to a costume shop and pick up a birthday crown and a set of rainbow suspenders. The student whose birthday it is will wear a piece of birthday finery on his or her special day.

2. Periodically, you make positive calls home. You have made a commitment to yourself that for every call home in which you inform a parent that a child is struggling, you make two positive calls home. After doing this a few times, you are amazed with the reactions. You feel marvelous after calling and saying "thank you" to a parent for encouraging their child in doing an exceptional job in class. You know students are aware that you call their homes with praise, and everyone wants to be next.

3. After watching a colleague you find creative ways to respond to students in class. You now incorporate the following into your interactions with students:

   "You're a hard worker. You can come up with the answer."

   "If you did know the answer, what would you say?"

   "It is physically impossible to talk and listen at the same time. What Joe has to say is so important that we need to hear it. Don't forget that you have two ears and only one mouth. Your ears outnumber your mouth; use your ears first."

   "You could have told me to leave you alone, but you didn't quit on me as your teacher. You care about success. Great job."

4. You show students respect with your actions and ask for the same from them. You never talk over noisy students and you do not use negative ways to get their attention. Instead, you move to the location you stood in at the beginning of the class, look at the class, and wait for them to quiet down. In addition, you talk to them as you would want them to talk to you.

5. When an off-task student needs redirected, you call him or her to the side and talk privately, one-on-one. This builds on the student-teacher relationship.

6. Overall, personalization is the key. Showing that you appreciate and find joy in your students is essential in keeping things positive.

Ways in Which Students Feel Motivated to Stretch Themselves:

Regardless of what students may say, they want to be challenged. Early in the year, after calling every student's home and getting a sense of each child's needs, you write personal and academic goals for each student. Over a period of few days, you devote class time to conference with each student. You decide to position the conference table in the corner of the classroom, so you can look over the head of the student to whom you are talking to and scan the rest of the class. (You know you can also bring in parents to monitor stations to keep the rest of the class on task.) During these five-minute conferences, you take notes and make sure the student does most of the talking. The purpose of these conversations is to get students to state their personal and academic goals for the year and then bring them up to yours. Every student needs to hear the guarantee that it's okay to be wrong, and they won't be in trouble for taking positive social and academic risks.

For students who are used to failing, you ask more pointed questions, like, "What is it going to take for you to care about your education?" You quickly follow this challenging comment with the reassurance that you will never quit on this student. A primary goal of education is for students to own their own lives and strive for excellence. A true professional broadens students' horizons so they can discover and develop parts of their futures they didn't know existed. And fostering student responsibility for their own lives is the best way to keep things positive.

➜ WHAT IS YOUR NEXT MOVE?—P. 73

Student Contract: Behavior and Academics

You are not participating in our class incentive today, because:

1. You have chosen to not do your academic work.
2. Your behavior is not respectful to our class environment.
3. You have not come in at lunch or after school for help.

This form is a contract, an agreement that we won't have this problem again.

Why do you think you are not participating today? _____

_____

_____

If you had to do this quarter again, what would you have done differently so you could have earned

your invitation? _____

_____

_____

Positive Incentives

What additional incentives would you like once you decide to do your work? Please circle all that you would like:

- ▶ Positive call home

- ▶ "Caught you doing something good" yellow slip to go first in line at lunch

- ▶ Preferential seating—you get to sit where you like

- ▶ One bathroom pass

- ▶ Other—please write your idea: _____

   _____

Negative Consequences

If you continue to not do your work or not respect our learning environment, these are the consequences:

- ▶ First time . . . . Negative call home

- ▶ Second time . . . . . . Beautification cleaning up the school

- ▶ Third time . . . . Yellow detention form

- ▶ Fourth time. . . . . . . Office referral

I will not give any more warnings. If you are having a rough time in your life, talk with me and I'll give you the space you need.

You are not a victim. You can control yourself and do your work. If the work is too much, you can talk with me and I can make adjustments to suit your needs. But you have to talk with me.

I hereby agree to both the Positive Incentives and Negative Consequences listed above:

_____   _____
Student's Name   Teacher's Name

Date: _____

Once the student is finishing the work and respecting our learning environment, on the following date we will reevaluate this contract and ideally treat this student just like any other student:

_____

8. Parent Conferences

IN preparing for parent conferences, other teachers at your school have offered you unsolicited advice covering the spectrum of orientations. Some say that parents don't care; some look forward to meeting with parents; some just want to get through the conferences as part of their job. You find yourself with questions: What is the purpose behind parent conferences?

In any case, you can't wait to meet with the parents of some students—especially the ones that subject your class to daily outbursts of drama. What you don't immediately realize is that you are just as much under the microscope as the parent and the student. Back-to-School Night was your coming-out party. Parent conferences are your job interview. Will you pass the community's scrutiny? Fundamentally, how much social capital and trust can you generate?

By the end of the conference, what will the continuing conversation at home sound like? "You're lucky to have that teacher this year. You'd better step up your work." or "You were right, honey. At least you have some other good teachers this year. Just make it through this year. Hopefully things will be better next year."

Your mentor teacher's voice rings in your head: "I have the privilege or working with your child for the next nine months. You have the privilege of being with your child for the next fifty years. Your child has the privilege of advocating for themselves for the next ninety years. How can we work together so your child can thrive?" Yeah, you might be able to use that. How can you weave that in to your conversations with parents? Before you choose to tackle student problems, always decide whether you would like for the student to be present along with the parent, or talk to parents and student separately.

How do you go about embracing your own version of "Meet the Parents"? You:

1. Find the parent conference goes well—p. 90
2. Have never spoken to the parent before—p. 90
3. Made your phone calls home, and are now just continuing conversations—p. 91
4. Don't have anything positive to say about the child—p. 92
5. Suspect the child is being abused—p. 93
6. Have a parent try to pick a fight—p. 95
7. Have parents confide in you that they are lost—p. 96
8. Have a parent who knows only half-truths about what is going on in your classroom—p. 97

Following is a discussion of each option. You can move from one to the next, or you can jump between options at any time.

Option 1. The Parent Conference Goes Well

"**WELCOME,**" you say to the parent and student in front of you. "Thank you for investing the time to be here. Your child has made tremendous progress this year, overcoming struggles and getting closer to academic proficiency. I'm open to following your lead during this conference, but I want to make sure we cover the wonderful growth socially and academically that he has made this year."

Now, the ball is on her side of the court, and you quietly take notes. The parent showed up to be heard more than hear from you. You want the parent to want to come back, so you let her talk, and you keep your comments to one minute to each of her five. You make a mental note that the reason this conference is going so well is because you are prepared. Your knowledge of the student is current and accurate, and you came with student work to prove the student's ongoing growth and resiliency.

Read body language during the conference to identify if you are nurturing or neglecting each stakeholder's sense of self-worth. You know that some signs to watch for are relaxed posture and good eye contact, and you see those here.

Closing out a parent conference with everyone's egos intact enables each participant to feel successful. Creating a win-win-win is the ultimate goal. You feel as though you leave the meeting with a "win" when your professionalism is respected and supported by the student's home. In the same way, parents need to close off the conference feeling like a valued partner in their child's education. Most of all, the student exits the meeting feeling appreciated for his success so far and driven for future success. You know that a parent conference is successful if you see each participant leave with head up rather than head down.

The parent and student rise to leave, heads held high. Your interaction has fired on all of these cylinders, and you feel good about having fostered an inclusive classroom where parents feel valued.

→ HOW DO YOU HANDLE THINGS NEXT?—P. 89

Option 2. You Have Never Spoken to the Parent Before

YOU started the year with good intentions. When you heard from a colleague that calling each student's home and introducing oneself has made a world of difference in student productivity, you were intrigued. But time at the beginning of the school year seemed to slip away. Expected and unexpected events interrupted the fulfillment of your goals—an exciting end to the baseball season; a family member needed hours of counseling; spontaneous invitations to get together with friends. All of these and more are incredibly valuable to you in embracing life, but you need balance to feel successful both personally and professionally.

So, as much as you wanted to, you did not get to make those phone calls, and you are going to meet your students' parents tonight for the first time. One is approaching you right now. You wonder what impression she has of you. The fact of the matter is the first impression you give of yourself and read in others is instantaneous and quite often beyond your control. As Princeton psychologists Janine Willis and Alexander Todorov found in 2006, it takes only a tenth of a second to make an impression.

You feel the butterflies in your stomach as the parent approaches. Breathe. You are acutely aware that you are in a job interview. You decide to use this parent conference as the opportunity to learn, not judge. Support and build, not preach and discard.

You chime in first, "How would you like to start?"

"What do you know about my child?" she demands. "What does my child need to do this year in your class?"

You look her in the eye and say, "We can spend our time together reading over the syllabus to answer your question, or you can tell me about your child's needs. My overall goal is for every student to thrive in my classroom. What would you like for me to know about your son so I can help him thrive?"

Because you have chosen to remain calm, you radiate confidence. When the parent opens up, you listen for the majority of your time together, and you feel assured that you passed this interview. You have helped to establish a joint effort. When the parent debriefs with the student at home, your social status elevates because you listened here.

→ HOW DO YOU HANDLE THINGS NEXT?—P. 89

Option 3. You Made Your Calls Home, and Are Now Just Continuing Conversations

BECAUSE you made your phone calls home, introduced yourself to parents, and actively listened to each parent, your own affective filter is dramatically lowered for parent conference week. You are amazed at how many hugs you get. Everyone knows that actions speak louder than words, and your actions illustrated how much you care about your students. You lose track of how many times you hear the parents say, "Thank you for calling home. No teacher has ever done that before," and "It is great to meet you."

All you did was try to build community. You took the advice of a colleague, who advised you to call every home at the beginning of the school year. (See Chapter 6 on page 57 for more information, and for the Student Information Sheet used in these calls). And because you have already invested in creating community with your students' parents, these conference times free you to have meaningful discussions.

Your time with the parent is now substantial. Stakeholders' affective walls are lowered. There is no doubt you are all committed to the students' success. The beauty of already being oriented to one another is that the face-to-face meeting can be about specific milestones and goals for the student. The conversation has substance.

→ HOW DO YOU HANDLE THINGS NEXT?—P. 89

Option 4. You Don't Have Anything Positive to Say About the Child

IN preparing for this particular parent conference, you are hard-pressed to think of something positive to say about this parent's child. You try to be a compassionate, rooting-for-the-underdog, inclusive person. But with this student? At the drop of a hat, you can list dozens of other students who have either been threatened or insulted by the student you are looking at right now across the conference table. You try not to think of all of the school resources that have been invested in trying to "rescue" this unmotivated, intransient child. Yes, you know you shouldn't think of students this way, but from your vantage point, this is what is honestly going on.

Is there a work ethic? You have lost track of how many reminder notices, telephone calls, and individual conversations you have had to help this child become more of a producer than a consumer. The dismal amount of work that he has turned in is too far below grade level to even be measured as academic achievement. This student and, apparently, this family are not sold on the importance of following your program.

Where do you start? How can you guide this conversation to clarify the rationale behind your high standards and the fact that the child is not meeting a single one of them without decimating any possible connection you can salvage with the student's family?

So you sit there looking at parent and child. Where do you start?

Empathy Break

And what can you say that is positive about this child? Well, for all of his troubles, he still comes to school. He now has an adult with him who cares enough to be here. There must be a part of this child who wants to do well, but he is lost on how to get there. And this adult is probably lost on how to help this child, which is a problem, because the biggest impact on anyone's life is what happens at home. You think about the fact that you are his pseudo rudder for a journey in the crosswinds of his life.

At this point, the easiest thing to do would be to convey the list of social and academic atrocities this child has committed in the short amount of time you have had the displeasure of knowing him. Now you breathe. Do you really want to inscribe your name in the child's long list of people who have embarrassed him? You are better than this. An educator brings out the best he or she can in *every* child.

Don't quit. You decide that instead of casting stones, you will try to build bridges. You are clear that you will continue holding the child accountable and you will not compromise your standards in your dealings with this young man.

What you say sounds like this: "First of all, thank you for coming. I need to be very direct with you. So far this year, your child has not performed up to his ability. Instead of my listing everything that has gone wrong, I would us to talk about how we can work together to make things right. What do you think your child needs at school so I can best serve your family?"

The parent will most likely give you a blank stare. If the parent knew what the child needed, she probably would have already done it. Your goal right now is to help bring the parent out. She is probably equally or more nervous than you are. The calmer and more reassuring you are, the more the parent may match the behavioral standard you set.

So there you are, facing a parent whose child you can't stand. You try again: "I'm here to help. We have a long road ahead of us. I would like your child to develop routines centered on success at school."

You then give the parent the student handout you have gone over in class every day since school began. (See the handout at the end of this chapter). You talk through the handout. If the parent leaves with a personalized action plan for their child utilizing these ten steps, you've done your job.

→ HOW DO YOU HANDLE THINGS NEXT?—P. 89

Option 5. You Suspect the Child is Being Abused

YOU have had trouble sleeping for several nights. Tonight are parent conferences, and your first one is with Katie's father.

You sensed something about Katie, but you haven't been able to articulate it. She has missed 20 percent of school days so far. Missing only a day a week enables her to check out and still fly under the school's radar. She has learned early how to manipulate the system. It won't be until April or May, when she has more than twenty absences, that anyone will notice, and then nothing will happen because it will be too late in the school year. When you looked at her cumulative folder, you found that she has squeaked by with C's over the past few years—not low enough to be considered at risk. She is a ghost walker. She is there but she is not.

When she is there, you try to watch for signs of . . . you don't know what. You would like to develop empathy for this child. You certainly can't connect with someone you don't understand, and effective teaching is all about connections.

Then you saw your first sign. Like most pivotal events, this sign might have seemed random to the outside observer. The reason it stood out to you was simply because you were looking.

You remember from your credential program that you should notice when students wear long sleeves in hot weather. A few weeks into the school year, Katie wore long sleeves, and the weather was warm. She had just returned from another elective four-day weekend. On that rare moment she reached out to borrow a pen from another student, the fabric on her sleeve pulled back. You saw a glimpse, your first one ever, of her damaged forearm. Was it a burn mark? Was it a cut? There was definitely a bruise. Almost as quickly as you saw the mark, she pulled down his sleeve. Did anyone else see it? You are sure you saw something.

As both an ethical adult and as a responsible community representative who works with children, you are required by law to report your suspicion of child abuse. You had always thought that you would have no qualms making such a report. Now you find yourself frozen and filled with self-doubt. What if you are wrong? Didn't you hear through the grapevine that Katie's father is a community leader? Will reporting backfire on you?

You decide to do some research. After a brief Internet search, you come across a report released in 2010 by the Children's Bureau of the U.S. Department of Health and Human Services. Some blurbs from the report become immediately seared in your memory:

> Three-quarters of unique victims had no history of prior victimization for each year from 2006 through 2010.

The youngest children are the most vulnerable to maltreatment. More than one-third (34.0%) of all 2010 unique victims were younger than 4 years. One-fifth (23.4%) of victims were in the age group 4–7 years.

Children younger than 1 year had the highest rate of victimization at 20.6 per 1,000 children in the population of the same age. Victims with the single-year age of 1, 2, or 3 years old had victimization rates of 11.9, 11.4, and 11.0 victims per 1,000 children of those respective ages in the population. In general, the rate and percentage of victimization decreased with age.

Victimization was split between the sexes, with boys accounting for 48.5 percent and girls accounting for 51.2 percent.

Four-fifths (78.3%) of unique victims were neglected, 17.6 percent were physically abused, 9.2 percent were sexually abused, 8.1 percent were psychologically maltreated, and 2.4 percent were medically neglected. In addition, 10.3 percent of victims experienced such "other "types of maltreatment as "abandonment," "threats of harm to the child," or "congenital drug addiction."

Four-fifths (81.3%) of victims were maltreated by a parent either acting alone or with someone else. Nearly two-fifths (37.2%) of victims were maltreated by their mother acting alone. One-fifth (19.1%) of victims were maltreated by their father acting alone. One-fifth (18.5%) of victims were maltreated by both parents. Thirteen percent of victims were maltreated by a perpetrator who was not a parent of the child (Children's Bureau, 2010).

After reading the report, you are even more concerned about Katie. Someone could indeed be hurting her, but what if she were hurting herself? You are aware that some young people can become addicted to cutting themselves.

You know you are required to report your suspicions within twenty-four hours, but before going to the authorities, you decide to talk to your guidance counselor. If the counselor is busy, you resolve to talk to the secretary in the front office. You know that any of these professionals can help you through the reporting process. If no one at school can help you, you know you will have to call Child Protective Services yourself.

You made your report a few weeks ago. All you have heard from the administration is that Child Protective Services is still looking into the case. Today, you are scheduled to meet with Katie's father. With what you know now, what will you say to him?

You spend the school day going through the motions at school, with your focus on the coming parent conference. You decide to not be alone. You ask at the main office, and you find that you can have an administrator sit next to you during the conference. If pressed by the parent, the administrator can simply say that sitting in on parent conferences is part of your evaluation. Another option is to ask one of Katie's other teachers to sit with you for a joint conference.

The administrator advises you that, during the meeting, you should not bring up the suspected abuse unless you clear it with the administration first. Let Child Protective Services run the investigation. Stay out of it. Focus on academics. You have done what you can to help.

➡ HOW DO YOU HANDLE THINGS NEXT?—P. 89

Option 6. A Parent Tries to Pick a Fight

"WHAT you are saying about my daughter is not true!" the parent in front of you screams. Everyone in the crowded multimedia center, where the parent conferences take place, is looking at you and this parent, who is standing over you, fuming. You think to yourself, "What did I say?"

"How dare you judge my child?" the parent continues. "Youhave only had her in your class for two months!"

Going into parent conferences, you need to be ready to respond to anything that may come your way. If a parent blows up at you, either one or two things will happen: you will see it coming or you won't. You can protect yourself from being blindsided by a parent if you find out all you can about your students before conferences. Even then, though, a parent may act unpredictably.

Before you respond, you try to take a moment to breathe and think. This parent wouldn't be here if she didn't want her child to succeed. You wait for the parent to pause in her tirade. It is critical that the first words out of your mouth be "I" statements that emphasize your empathy and your listening skills.

"I can hear that you feel as though your child is not being served well in my classroom," you say. You are conscious that at the moment you are being evaluated, not only by the parent ranting at you, but also by any and all spectators. The last thing you want to do is lose your cool. After the parent says more hurtful things at you, you sit patiently. Let her vent, while you stay serene. "I heard you raise some serious things for us to talk about," you say. "Which topic would you like me to respond to first?"

As you keep the conversation focused on constructive ways in which you and the parent can help each other, you recall a poem by Mother Teresa, "Do it Anyway":

People are often unreasonable, irrational, and self-centered. Forgive them anyway.

If you are kind, people may accuse you of selfish, ulterior motives. Be kind anyway.

What you spend years creating, others could destroy overnight. Create anyway.

The good you do today, will often be forgotten. Do good anyway.

Give the best you have, and it will never be enough. Give your best anyway.

In the final analysis, it was never between you and them anyway."

→ HOW DO YOU HANDLE THINGS NEXT?—p. 89

Option 7. Parents Confide in You That They Are Lost

IN one conference, a parent that you know well says, "Could you just tell me what to do, so if things go wrong I have someone to blame?" She has said this mostly tongue-in-cheek. She is thankfully more direct than the average guarded parent, but she has spoken an absolute truth from most parents' points of view. Schools can appear to be metaphorical and literal jungles. More times than not, the parents are more afraid of you than you are of them.

In another conference, a parent says to you, "I'm really lost. I don't know what to do. My child seems out of control. What would you do?" You have a few choices here:

1. Crush the parent's little heart and tell him or her that the child is hopeless.
2. Be oblivious and unresponsive.
3. Be real, be present, and be optimistic.

Above all, cut each parent some slack. Parenting is often a rough, thankless task. It is a comprehensive effort to guide, set limits, be nurturing, selfless, and not spineless. People really do the best they can with what they know. Your job as an educator is not to lose sight of your primary mission—serving the student. To accomplish that mission, you need to help ground and buttress this wayward parent. Remember, reflective listening and empathy are the keys to building a communal effort.

"I hear your frustration," you say. "What do you think your child needs?" With that question, you anticipate that the parent may put some of the burden of those needs on you. Stand your ground. You expect the parent to work with you, not leave all the work to you. Also, try to get to the root of the problem and identify how to break up responsibilities.

During the course of your conversation, respectfully guide the parent to come to his or her own solutions as to how to best help the child. The moment you tell the parent what to do, the problem and its outcome become your responsibility. It is in the best interest of the child, the parent, and the whole family dynamic that they own their problem and the process of how to fix it. Humor aside, you need to sidestep any landmine such as, "Could you just tell me what to do, so if things go wrong I have someone to blame?"

→ HOW DO YOU HANDLE THINGS NEXT?—P. 89

Option 8. A Parent Knows Only Half-Truths About What is Going on in Your Classroom

"NO, I never said that!" you scream in your head. "How can these parents really believe what their child says about me? Wow! What did I do to offend her so badly that she wants to manipulate her parents against me?"

You are a professional in a professional setting, a parent conference, so you sit taking notes on each of this student's unfounded allegations about how you are under-serving her. You look at the child sitting across the table from you. You look for some of Marc Salem's (2008) clues that someone is lying:

- She is compulsively licking her lips before speaking.
- When you press her for specifics, she squirms.
- She is leaving long pauses as she speaks, like she's making it up as she goes along.
- She is hiding her hands under the table.
- Her pupils are dilated—a sure clue!

You decide to handle this in the same way you treated the angry parent: ride it out. You take notes throughout the diatribe while maintaining eye contact as much as you can. You pause for reflective listening, but ask plenty of questions for clarification. With enough questions, the truth will come out.

Once the parent gets upset, which will happen much sooner rather than later, you can be the first one to suggest that you bring in an administrator to help mediate the problem. When you do eventually sit down with the administrator, you can rightfully say that all you did was ask questions. If you have acted negligently, you must be the first one to step forward, own up, and pave the way for moving on. The best leadership embraces honesty.

If the parent is conspiring against you, be patient. You can only control you. The truth will always come out.

Important Note

Stay away from exaggeration, such as, "It sounds as though I am doing a horrible job in my classroom." Instead, say, "I heard that you brought up quite a few concerns. Overall, it sounded to me that you two think I am under-serving your child."

Keep all of your comments specific to the student in front of you. Don't bring up other students unless it is absolutely critical to the discussion. You never want to be seen as a gossip-monger. The calmer and cooler you are, the more power you have.

Above all, keep your emotions in check. Their view of you does not determine who you are.

→ HOW DO YOU HANDLE THINGS NEXT?—P. 89

The Ten Steps of How I Can Be Successful

1. **Be Here.** Successful people go to work regularly. They tend to work longer hours than less successful people. Remember, right now, your school is your work.

2. **Be On Time.** People who are successful get to where they are going on time. Others count on them to be where they say they are going to be, when they say they are going to be there.

3. **Be Friendly.** No violence. Successful people become successful because they help each other, not because they hurt each other. Successful people build or create. Unsuccessful people destroy by doing physical or spoken violence. To be friendly is to accept the differences of others.

4. **Be Polite.** Successful people are polite people. They know that other people help them to be successful, so they treat others with respect. They listen when others are talking. They wait their turn. They consider the feelings of others. They wait to be called on in class.

5. **Be Prepared.** Bring your tools and supplies to class. Successful people take good care of their equipment and they have the equipment they need when they go to work.

6. **Be A Listener.** Successful people listen to instructions and follow directions. By listening, successful people hear what others need so they can cooperate for success.

7. **Be A Doer.** Do your work the best you can. Successful people are doers. They know more they do more they will know how to do. Good baseball players become good baseball players because they play a whole lot of baseball.

8. **Be A Tough Worker.** Keep trying. Successful people keep working even when things get difficult. When the going gets tough the tough get going. Tough times never last but successful people do.

9. **Be A Risk Taker.** Show courage. Stick your neck out. Ask questions. Successful people are willing to run the risk of failure because they know that sooner or later they will make it if they keep trying.

10. **Be A Success.** Successful people are achievers. They complete their projects, turn them in on time, and feel good when they have finished their work.

From B. David Brooks, PhD, and Robert C. Paull, PhD, at the Thomas Jefferson Research Center

9. IEP Meetings

SCHOOLS are required to perform an annual review of each special education student's Individual Education Plan, or IEP. Ethically and legally, schools are required to do as much as they can to help all students demonstrate proficiency in all academic subjects. The goal is to empower the student and the student's family to feel secure, supported, and challenged. Because every teacher is in one way or another affected by the school's special education program, you decide to do your own research. You find information on the website of the New America Foundation's Federal Education Budget Project (2012):

> The Individuals with Disabilities Education Act (IDEA) is the main federal statute that authorizes federal aid for the education of more than 6 million children with disabilities nationally. The statute has two key components: (1) due process provisions detailing parental rights, and (2) a permanently authorized grant program that provides federal funding to the states. States that receive federal funds are required to provide a "free, appropriate public education" to all children with disabilities in the "least restrictive environment."

As a new teacher, you have already heard the phrase "least restrictive environment" many times. Your goal is to help all students achieve proficiency in all academic subjects and to nurture appropriate social development in all students. The cognitive development of special education students is just as essential as that of any other student. However, nothing is free. The financial toll of special education programs on school districts is staggering, according to the Federal Education Budget Project (2012):

> Local school districts have had trouble covering such a high percentage of the $50 billion spent on special education services. Heavily impacted districts with a disproportionate number of high-need, high-cost disabled students struggle the most, particularly if the district is small or rural. Of all disabled students, approximately one-half of one percent, or around 330,000 students, require more than $100,000 in special education services per year.

Taken as a whole, local governments need to fulfill expanded statutory obligations with less funding. In part because of funding restrictions, you may witness a push to exit more and more students out of special education classes.

Mainstreaming special education students into general education classes helps all school stakeholders develop into more empathic, socially inclusive adults. In other words, mainstreaming is good for the entire school, adults and students alike. However, inclusion is rarely easy. Special education students often have substantial needs; that is why they are in special education. In addition, the parents need help to best support their child.

Your challenge is to help every stakeholder succeed. As you enter your first special education meeting, you think of a litany of options and possibilities:

- How can you best support your special needs student?
- What support does the family need?
- Which services can the school provide?
- How can these services be measured to make sure the accommodations are working?
- Essentially, how can you improve your practice so *all* of your students can become proficient in your subject area?

What is your next move? You:

1. Miss the meeting, which happened the previous day—p. 100
2. Confuse the student with another student—p. 100
3. Develop an eye to unify messages—p. 101
4. Find the psychologist blames you for the student's difficulties—p. 102
5. Check in with the student—p. 104

Following is a discussion of each option. You can move from one to the next, or you can jump between options at any time.

Option 1. You Miss the Meeting, Which Happened the Previous Day

YOU saunter into the main office, geared up for your meeting. You have already thought out what you want to say and how you want to be encouraging. You even have sample work to buttress the points you want to make.

The secretary looks at you quizzically. "May I help you?"

"Yes, thank you. Has the special education meeting already started in the conference room?"

"Yes," she says. "The meeting started and finished. Yesterday."

In all of your earnestness to be thoughtful, thorough, and together—and you missed it. As with all new teachers, a common mistake appears to take on life-or-death importance. You leave the main office in search of the special education caseworker who ran yesterday's meeting. When you find her, she is busy working with another student's family. When she comes in pursuit of you, you are busy teaching. After a few more near connections, which turn into near misses, you finally seek out five minutes to go over the notes concerning your student.

After you apologize profusely for missing the meeting, she gives you a look that can only be interrupted as "Get over yourself. I have more important things to worry about." She gladly gives you the updated notes outlining the current learning objectives and appropriate accommodations from yesterday's meeting.

→ WHAT IS YOUR NEXT MOVE?—P. 100

Option 2. You Confuse the Student with Another Student

IT is early in the school year. Preparing for and implementing your classes has already taken a physical toll. By the end of September, when your first wave of IEP meetings starts, you are *tired*. This is the long way of saying you will probably mess up.

Halfway through your talk at the IEP meeting, you realize that not only did you bring in the wrong student's work samples (which you haven't shown yet—thank goodness), you also confused this student with one of your other special education students. How can you backtrack and save face?

Three words—Honestly Own Up: "I'm so sorry. I know Henry and his work in my class. Unfortunately, I mistakenly grabbed a different student's work samples. Let me go back through and restate my observations about Henry's academic and social development."

Teaching is a human-relations-based endeavor. The moment you come to terms with your humanity and toss away any pretense of knowing all of the answers, the more accepting your school community will be of you. In the same way you expect your students to embrace the challenge of taking on new risks, you need to open yourself up to messing up. You are human.

→ WHAT IS YOUR NEXT MOVE?—P. 100

Option 3. You Develop an Eye to Unify Messages

ONE of your first IEP meetings will be for Michael, a student in your class. Michael does not appear to be emotionally invested in his work. Instead he seems to feel adrift. You are not well versed in what happens in an IEP meeting, so you are not certain what you will present in Michael's meeting.

First you realize you need a wider vision of scene. Because you want to be prepared for your first meeting, you continue to do your own research. You find a treasure trove of information on the website of the Disability Rights Education and Defense Fund. The site outlines the steps that a school takes to move students through the IEP process. It explains eligibility and defines an IEP and its annual review. You feel much better informed after the time you spend reading this site.

You attend the IEP meeting, knowing how important it is to both Michael and his family. You are not experienced in attending these meetings, and you want to observe for a while. When your time comes to share your insights about Michael, you ask if you can go later. You tell other participants, "I'm really interested in learning more from the perspective of the other people around the table."

When your time comes again, you measure your responses against what has already been shared. You respect the student and his family too much to not speak frankly. You focus your talking points on specific data. You bring in work samples to highlight academic needs. You talk encouragingly about specific examples of success—social and academic—that Michael has shown. You find that the same themes come up again and again for him. You tie your comments into themes you heard expressed in the room. By doing so, you help knit together the tapestry of Michael's current progress across the spectrum of school life. Thus, it is easier to map out a specific course for Michael to succeed into the future.

→ WHAT IS YOUR NEXT MOVE?—P. 100

Option 4. The Psychologist Blames You for the Child's Difficulties

THIS IEP is being treated as an annual check-in. The student is not making substantial progress in terms of quantifiable academic achievement. However, there seems to be a consensus between the parents and the teachers that continuing the existing mainstreaming schedule serves the student's need to mature socially. Across the conference table, you see the child's psychologist, whom the parents brought to the meeting. He appears to be holding in anger and bursting to speak.

Suddenly, you hear him burst out with a warning to the parents, "I would not sign off on maintaining this program. This school can give both you and Michael better services."

"What are you referring to?" you ask.

The psychologist stares directly at you. "None of Michael's developmental needs are being met in your classroom," he barks.

Your fight reflex is winning the battle of control over your flight reflex. Breathe.

"Are you basing your assessment on the five minutes you once spent observing in my classroom?" You recall the psychologist's fleeting visit to your classroom the previous week.

"As a professional, I know when students' needs are being met in a classroom," he sneers. He then turns to the parents. "If I were you, I would ask to change Michael's schedule so his needs can be fully met. Then you can sign an agreement that the IEP is meeting Michael's needs."

Is this really happening? Did he really just publically say that you were deficient in meeting your student's needs? Breathe. One naysayer does not frame your identity. Your gaze never veers from him.

"Please tell me how I can improve my practice," you say to him. You are secure enough that you can hear professional criticism without taking a mortal blow to your sense of self-worth. You can see the psychologist's shoulders lower. "Wow," he says. "I thought you would just be defensive." His body language is now more relaxed and open. "Do you really want to know? Teaching modifications for special education students is simply just good teaching. All best practices stem out of knowing your clientele. How can we set up every classroom to center around equity so every student, including Michael, can achieve to the best of their ability?

"The National Dissemination Center for Children with Disabilities has a list of ideas for modifications." The psychologist takes out his iPhone and brings up the website, which shows the following list:

- ▶ Scheduling. For example,
  - ▷ giving the student extra time to complete assignments or tests
  - ▷ breaking up testing over several days
- ▶ Setting. For example,
  - ▷ working in a small group
  - ▷ working one-on-one with the teacher
- ▶ Materials. For example,
  - ▷ providing audiotaped lectures or books
  - ▷ giving copies of teacher's lecture notes
  - ▷ using large print books, Braille, or books on CD (digital text)

- ▸ Instruction. For example,
    - ▹ reducing the difficulty of assignments
    - ▹ reducing the reading level
    - ▹ using a student/peer tutor
- ▸ Student Response. For example,
    - ▹ allowing answers to be given orally or dictated
    - ▹ using a word processor for written work
    - ▹ using sign language, a communication device, Braille, or native language if it is not English.

"I would go beyond these initial simple adjustments," the psychologist elaborates. "Let's go deeper and personalize this discussion to best fit Michael's needs following the NCCD outline:

"First, scheduling: By the end of the day, Michael is on information overload. We should change his schedule so he has P.E. and his elective class after lunch. Because Michael is a logical-mathematical thinker, his most difficult class, language arts, should take place when he can focus best—second period. During first period, he is still adjusting to his day at school, so he should start his day with math—his strongest subject.

"Now, setting: In each class, Michael needs as many opportunities to access the information as possible. Setting matters. It is often assumed that students in the front rows get the better grades. Quite often that is true. But this really depends on the teacher. We need to put Michael where he can have the best vantage point for each teacher. For his math and language arts teachers, sitting in the front row will help since those teachers don't move around the class very often. In social studies class, Mr. Michaels is all over the room because his instruction is more dynamic. Michael's desk should be in the center of the room so he can absorb the spectrum of Mr. Michaels's instruction. What I am saying is that blanket statements rarely work. Intimate knowledge of each instructional setting is the gold standard. All of this being said, our goal should be to nurture Michael's independence. Starting in second semester, he should be challenged to change desks often so he can be more flexible to his learning environment.

"Next, materials: Like all people, Michael finds organization to be a constant battle. Maintaining effective organization is a minute-by-minute obstruction. We have all seen Michael's answer to organization: he crams his work in his backpack—that is, if he has his backpack with him that day. The simple solution is to take 20 seconds at the end of each class period to help him put his materials away carefully. One seven-pocket accordion file is an ideal way for each student to discretely organize handouts in separate folders as papers are passed out. One pocket per class. Make sure to offer help if necessary.

"In terms of instruction and student response: The best teachers use a wide spectrum of presentation and review strategies. Teaching to multiple learning modalities should be the norm, not the exception. For every lesson, previewing your instruction enables all students to thrive. Unquestionably, students see you as a role model. Open yourself up. Before you start your instruction, tell students how long you will be talking for—and always try to keep that time to less than ten minutes at a stretch. Ideally, for every five minutes of lecture time, you should ask students a 'checking in' question to discuss with a partner. These thirty-second interludes enable you to walk around the classroom and check in with your special education students and English language learners. To reach higher levels of inclusion, take your checking-in to the public stage. Tell students the question you will ask them and make sure they know the answer. This type of inclusion enables all students to practice demonstrating competency in a public forum. If you give a student the privilege of 'passing,' make sure you come back and ask him or her a follow-up question within three minutes of any 'pass.'

"You asked how we can modify the school experience so Michael can be most successful. If all of these adaptations can be implemented, we can all work together to facilitate Michael's autonomy. Developing the habits of a successful mind takes practice and repetition."

The outcome of your open orientation to the psychologist's suggestions is that you effectively did your job. By focusing on improving your orientation to Michael, you learned how to improve your pedagogy for all students. Walking out of the meeting, you are proud of yourself.

➜ WHAT IS YOUR NEXT MOVE?—P. 100

Option 5. You Check In with the Student

YOU have heard from the psychologist, the parents, the school counselor, and the other teachers. Going to the source is the only way to know if all of this work is helping Michael thrive.

Because it is difficult for you to create time in your classroom for a leisurely follow-up conversation with Michael, and a hallway conversation doesn't feel adequate, you decide to invest in spending lunch time with Michael. From your life experience, you know that what was said to Michael during the IEP meeting was not necessarily what Michael heard. For growth to take hold, he needs to be a team player in his academic plan—for a fifteen-minute conversation. One-on-one time is critical for this child.

You start by modeling the honesty you want Michael to exhibit: "I'm here to help. You won't offend me, nothing bad will happen if you are honest with me. What is the truth? How often are you confused at school?" You have a flood of questions, but you know that bombarding Michael will only clog the conversation.

You spent most of his previous IEP meeting listening. Your contribution regarding his progress was important, pertinent, and honest. You decide to take the same approach with Michael now. Being a listener during this time is most important to create a connection, which is on Michael's terms, so he is invested in caring about his education.

At times, you need to add a little fuel to keep the conversational fire alight. Reflective listening is the key. You repeat back what Michael says in your own words. This communicates to Michael that you care and are listening, and it helps you check that what he actually means what he says. You then launch your own questions:

> "What do you think of your progress? Why?"
>
> "What did you think of the IEP meeting?"
>
> "Did everything in the meeting go the way you wanted it to?"

You also offer him support by telling him the following:

1. You will never give up on him. Your stability is vital. By being a stable mentor, you can be his checking-in point. Chances are he will rarely reach out to you, but you are there. Michael can talk to you about the turmoil of being a child.
2. You will provide second chances on assignments. If the goal of school is attaining mastery, students should have multiple opportunities to correct their assignments. You decide that when you grade a paper, you will highlight what the student is doing well. This feedback is vital. The yellow highlight successes are the first thing that jump out at each student when they get papers back.

Second, instead of writing detailed comments about each student's writing error, all you do is write the number that corresponds with the common errors list stapled to the back of the page. Students then tabulate their errors. During the course of multiple assignments assigned during the semester, each student can quantify their growing writing proficiency by self-monitoring the decrease in common error events.

Third, each student can then fix his or her mistakes. On the back of each writing assignment, the students write the corrected version of their work. Pursuing mastery is doable with repetition, high expectations, and specific support.

If all goes right, you will leave the conversation with a deeper understanding of Michael's viewpoint regarding his own education. Even better, you will reassure Michael that he is not alone, second chances in life do exist, and that he can become the person he aspires to be.

→ WHAT IS YOUR NEXT MOVE?—P. 100

10. Nurturing Parental Involvement

"**THANK** you for your help. My son loves your class. If you need any help with anything, please tell me." You have heard several versions of this same refrain from multiple parents. Why do parents say this? Are they genuinely offering help? Or is this just an empty comment like, "Have a nice day?" The easy response is to accept politely: "Thank you, I will." What if you did take her seriously? What roles can parents play in your school?

You look around your school and you see good people. With a few exceptions, students are genuinely grateful to be there. Most of the teachers get along. Life could always be better, but you can imagine far worse. There is a general upward swing of student progress academically and socially. Of course, there are constant setbacks and issues, but on the whole, life isn't bad. During the course of your day, you try to think of ways to promote and propel this progress.

It is this interconnectedness and communal responsibility that brought you to being a teacher. The cornerstone of your "think beyond yourself" mentality is inclusivity. The problem for you is the reaches of inclusivity. You have had some success planning with other colleagues, and you have heard praise from several colleagues for how you empower students to work collaboratively and still be individually responsible.

But there is always more to be done. You want to welcome parents and other community members to come in and help, but how to best involve them? You know that parents' expectations for inclusion and role responsibilities usually stem from their own views of themselves and their communities. You also know that more affluent parents may be the ones with the time and freedom to help during the day, but they may also feel entitled to tell you what to do in your classroom. Less affluent parents may be so overwhelmed with their day-to-day responsibilities that they can't come in as often. You want to be fair about giving all parents the opportunity to help—but do you have the time to manage parent workers in your classroom?

You come to the conclusion that involving parents in your classroom is a common sense move, both for you and for your students. Fundamentally, by embracing community involvement, you pave the way for both students and parents to be involved in charting a more inclusive society. However, you know that there are potential issues you need to think through first:

What does parental involvement look like in your classroom? What do you have for them to do? And is that work interesting enough for them to want to continue helping you?

How can you make it clear to those parents that they cannot dictate everything you do? How do you handle conflicts and let-downs, both between them and you and between each other?

What tactics will you choose for preparing to bring in the parents? You:

1. Respond when a parent lets you down—p. 108
2. Set up the environment so all can succeed—p. 109
3. Scaffold parental involvement to match your curricular events—p. 110
4. Get the administration on board—p. 111
5. Handle a student who acts out in front of the parents—p. 112
6. Handle parents who have a fight in your classroom—p. 114

Following is a discussion of each option. You can move from one to the next, or you can jump between options at any time.

Option 1. Respond When a Parent Lets You Down

YOU are halfway through your school year. You have successfully completed three end-of-unit events, and you are feeling as though you can delegate more responsibilities to parents. You want to cover your bases, so you have utilized as many avenues as possible in soliciting parent support for your next in-class event. You sent a mass e-mail outlining your event and asking for parent involvement. You also posted a sign-up sheet in the community/news section bulletin board in your classroom.

You made sure, as always, to outline what assignments students needed to complete to earn the privilege of being invited to your event (see page 79). You have heard from many students that their parents love the frankness of expectations embedded in your instruction. Most of all, these students have told you how their parents have already told them to work hard so as to earn their invitation.

Your plan for the next event is to combine content with a service-learning project. The class will host a one-mile fun-run to raise money to buy new library books. There will be several ripple effects of this unit. Because you teach science, students need to complete their physiology unit to earn the privilege of being part of this event. As a language arts tie-in, you also expect them to write a short story about the life of a ligament. To teach field research skills, you have assigned your students homework that involves surveying other students throughout the school and creating a list of books that other students would be interested in reading. Within a week, your students have come up with a fairly sizeable list of sought-after titles for your school library. You have even brought in a secretary from the main office to do a fifteen-minute lecture on purchase orders, the list of school-district-approved booksellers, and calculating the costs of the books students want to buy. That has brought in basic math and a real-world application.

When you first thought up this unit, you immediately questioned the time commitment. You have found that having students work for a larger community purpose motivates them to work more efficiently. The race deadline and the purchase order deadline are immovable. You were dumbfounded when students finished their homework and took on additional responsibilities because they knew other students in their school were watching their progress. You even saw a group of students start the process of a massive book exchange with neighboring schools, while another found sponsors for the event. Delegating responsibilities to parents seemed like an easy tie in.

On the morning of the run, you decide to conduct a mock race registration process. All seems well until you look for the parent in charge of the water station. What you find is no cups, no water, and no parent.

Thankfully, there are two parents on hand to handle pre-race registration, which gives you a five-minute window to make frenetic phone calls. You humbly ask the afterschool sports coach for a cooler and cups. No help. You frantically call the main office. No help. Finally, one of the science teachers finds an old cooler in the back closet. You scramble to the cafeteria to ask for fifty cups, enough to cover one class with a handful of cups left over.

Your feel embarrassed, rushed, and disorganized. You are tempted to lash out at the flakey parent for this near disaster. It is hard to keep in mind that fundamentally, this is your class and anything that emanates from it is your responsibility.

Over the next few days, you are simmering inside. How should you deal with this flakey parent? Quite possibly, the parent knows she left you in a lurch and is too embarrassed to call you. More than anything, you are kicking yourself. This is the same parent who never called you back after you called students' homes at the beginning of the school year. Come to think of it, she has never responded to your notes home, nor has she signed any of her child's homework. With all of these warning signs, why didn't you develop a backup plan?

Although you are tempted to send this parent a strongly worded e-mail message, you breathe. You remember that e-mails never die. If you ever see this parent again, you will need to rise above your disdain.

Lesson learned. Be inclusive and appreciative of parental support, but be cautious. Everyone is busy. If you are hosting the event, the event is yours to host.

➜ WHAT TACTIC WILL YOU TRY NEXT?—P. 107

Option 2. Set Up the Environment So All Can Succeed

YOU quickly come to the realization that you need to create a setting where parents and guardians have a vested interest in following through on their commitments. Is there anything you can do to set up the environment where everyone—parents, guardians, and students alike—are motivated to care?

Empathy Break

Remember that each one of the people you work has their own definition of success. Your definition of success may not match theirs. Hence, when you are frustrated at what appears to be a lack of effort to produce demonstrable involvement in your classroom, another person may feel as though they have done a great job. The parent who flaked on you at the water table may never have reached out to a classroom before. It may have taken a big effort for her to put her name out there to be involved. Her lack of responsibility is still unacceptable, but given a few more chances to be involved, she may demonstrate more responsibility.

So, here is your difficult balance between being inclusive of multiple interpretations of success and still maintaining your standards. So after a quick Web search, you come across Richard E. Clark's "Three Motivational Strategies That Work for Everyone" (Clark 2003):

1. **Help people develop self-confidence in their work skills**. Your interpretation of this insight is to help promote self-confidence; you need to know what individual parents' goals are. You have heard some general goals from them. "I want my child to do well," or "As long as my son stays out of trouble, this will be a good year," or "Just get good grades," or "I want them to make good friends." While all four of these generalities are important, once you can personalize what success means to each of the families you work with, you can modify parental involvement opportunities to be more meaningful for each family. Quite possibly, a mom or dad who fails to complete their allotted tasks just unintentionally picked a job that was not meaningful enough for them to follow through.

2. **Create a positive emotional environment at work**. Applying this second motivator is easy. Stay positive! Others will measure you by their first impression and last impression of you, but you never know when your last impression will happen. In other words, in order for you to set the stage for parental involvement, you will need to focus on the positive and catch people doing things right. You

can attract more bees with honey than with vinegar. The more humor and beneficial experiences you can create for all stakeholders in your classroom, the more they will want to come back for more.

3. **Support the development of strong personal values for performance goals**. Going through the motivational arc from number one, personalization, to number two, acceptance, it is only logical that you end with number three, recognition. Everyone reacts well when they feel as though their work is meaningful to the larger whole. The only way to convey that connection is through openness.

You find that investing the ten minutes to send out a mass e-mail that thanks parents and identifies exactly how person contributed to your event not only helps with event closure but also serves as a parent motivator for future events. To finish your work on the third motivator, you try to foster social connections. Ideally, parents who are successful in one job—such as snack organizer—can connect with and job-train another parent. Eventually, you will find that creating these social connections will elevate the social responsibility and create a web of support for your program and the community. Parents will start to recognize the value of each other through meaningful work in your classroom.

The more you set the stage for community involvement in your classroom, the more you see how complicated it can be. You keep in mind that you do not want to lose sight of the larger picture. Delegating responsibilities does not make parents your staff. As a teacher, you serve the community. Parents are your clients. You don't put them to work so you can do less. You put them to work so students benefit more.

→ WHAT TACTIC WILL YOU TRY NEXT?—P. 107

Option 3. Scaffold Parental Involvement to Match Your Curricular Events

PEOPLE want to be useful. According to the Corporation for National and Community Service, in 2010, 62.8 million adults volunteered almost 8.1 billion hours to various organizations. You would be grateful to see have some of those hours spent in your classroom, and you want to prepare for that.

For that to happen, you need to scaffold your year, breaking your curriculum into chunks. For each chunk, you need to brainstorm how parents can be a part of your program beyond performing simple clerical jobs. What are some of the bigger projects that you haven't had time to implement? Then you need to survey your parents. What skills do they have that you can adapt to your instructional needs?

For example, you have considered an event in which your class puts a fictional character on trial in order to highlight persuasion and motive. Are any of your parents attorneys? Their expertise would really add authenticity to this project. If you are covering the Renaissance, why not bring a parent who is an aspiring inventor, scientist, or computer programmer to discuss the creative and scientific process? And if you are covering the Great Depression, you can bring in any parent who may be willing to talk about the steps in a job search.

The intent behind this twist toward parent inclusion is to create a list of parents for your students to contact for surveys, experiential exercises, and other well-rounded research that goes beyond Internet searches. You will find that regardless of where or what you teach, there will be a wealth of community resources of which you may not have been aware.

Before you go public with your idea, you try to envision how the event will actually play out. You try to dissect the elements by answering a series of open-ended questions:

What are the particular meaningful details, which add meaning to the event?

What are the overarching life messages you want participants to personify, such as inclusion and developing a communal agenda, which is not just your agenda?

How does this event play into the larger themes of your year?

What are the curricular tie-ins? Why is this essential to your instruction? (This is a key question to help you justify parental inclusion).

What do participants need to do to prepare? (Try to make sure it is not to burdensome).

How much time will you allocate for the event? Will this time allocation conflict with other school activities or classes?

Are you up to any potential backlash from colleagues?

You need to seriously consider all of these questions so you will feel most comfortable with the parental involvement you invite into your work environment.

➜ WHAT TACTIC WILL YOU TRY NEXT?—P. 107

Option 4. Get the Administration on Board

YOU decide to talk to your principal about your plan to open your classroom to parent volunteers. Although your school has a School Site Council and a PTA, the level of involvement you have in mind is relatively new ground for your school. You see multiple opportunities for parents in your classroom, and you want to be open with your principal about that.

To prepare for this meeting, you decide to create a plan that states your case for community inclusion. Your list centers on one question: Who benefits?

Students: By being part of a synergy of purpose, students learn how parental collaboration works firsthand.

Parents: Within an inclusive school, parents are more able to synchronize school and home expectations through common experience, which reinforces student achievement.

Staff: By developing an expanding, supportive base, delegating responsibilities will be easier and more services will be available to help more people.

Community: Placing schools as the centerpiece of social networks brings people closer together. We all know that once you get to know someone through positive common experience, it is harder to dislike him or her.

School District: The more parents that take part in the positive running of schools, the easier it is to attain financing for bonds and parcel taxes in the future (Putnam 1993).

So, in your mind you are set. You are sufficiently prepared to start a conversation to explore expanding the role of parents on campus. You've done your research on motivation and the outcome of your plan.

Your principal's first response is not necessarily what you had hoped for. "The last thing we need is more parents on campus," she says, "We are here to work with students. You have no idea how much these parents are constantly breathing down my neck."

Empathy Break

Your principal is right: you have no idea how much energy she has to expend in dealing with community drama. Sometimes it is just easier to resist what is possible because the day-to-day rigors of life are overwhelming.

Your principal brings up an issue you hadn't considered: "You know, you need to protect yourself. According to state law, every parent needs to be fingerprinted to work alone with students. You need to monitor any parents you bring on campus. If something goes wrong, your reputation is on the line."

She is right. Cautious and conscientious planning needs to be your mantra. Before you can fully present the scope of your vision, your astute principal looks you in the eye and bluntly lays out her unmovable viewpoint, "We run this school. The school personnel run this school. Students might think they make the rules and try to bend us to their will. Parents will try everything in their power to bend us to their will. If you choose to bring more parents on this campus, I'll support you. But be mindful of what you are doing, because it could be a mine field."

After you leave her office, you realize that you never presented your carefully planned speech on the importance of community inclusion. However, you realize that you may not have needed it; she never said no.

When you do open your classroom, you must set specific limits for parents. You cannot lose sight of the fact that school personnel run the school. While parents may be too busy to be involved or want to tell you how to do your job, you will have to maintain the equilibrium to not engage in social drama. Most of all, you can never waver from your priority to put the students' need first.

➜ WHAT TACTIC WILL YOU TRY NEXT?—P. 107

Option 5. Handle a Student Who Acts Out in Front of the Parents

CONOR, who has barely earned his invitation to this end-of-unit event, now decides to take center stage and be a one-person wrecking crew. His mother, who is volunteering for this event, is on the other side of your classroom. She is either intentionally ignoring her son, or just plain oblivious.

Before you act, you survey the scene. Your timing is critical. Another thirty seconds of Conor being "on stage" and you will lose ten minutes trying to get your class back on track and refocused on your day's agenda. Like a flash of light, a list of options goes through your head:

1. Public chastisement: Yell, "Stop it!" Is that the modeling you want to exhibit for all of the parents to see? Doubtful, but possible. You already know that your previous attempts to put a lid on Conor only motivate him to act out more.

2. Grab Conor by the scruff of his neck and escort him out of your class: This could be tempting. Nothing else has gotten through to the student all year, and he is ruining what should be a beautiful day. Rough housing a child may eliminate the immediate problem but will only cause disastrous consequences for you tomorrow.

3. Double dip: Yell at the mom to yell at Conor. Once again, this could play out awesomely, giving everyone a cool story to tell, but you and the principal will then be putting out fires for weeks to come.

4. Bring out your inner Zen Master: The least exciting option is usually the best. You model the behavior you want others to follow.

Somewhat reluctantly, you go with Option 4. You calmly walk over to Conor's mother and ask her to step out of the classroom with you. On your way to the door, you veer over to Conor and politely ask him to step outside with you.

If Conor lashes out and escalates the scene, you must still remain serene. The mother is most likely on her way out the door, and she is well aware that you are not pleased. Depending on both Conor and his mother's ability to feel social shame, you will get them removed from the picture. You make a conscious commitment that you will not become emotional. If they flare out, it is their problem. All you did was ask them to step out of your room. In your head, you are ready to call in the principal, if need be. You are amazed by the beautiful power of social pressure. People want to conform. Acting out comes when conforming is too hard or not important. Most importantly, you will maintain your Zen vibe.

On the way out the door, you ask yourself why Conor was acting out. From your perspective, it comes down to one thing: limit setting. Although you have expressed your behavioral expectations to the entire class before any event in your room, Conor has had difficulty consistently holding up his end of the social contract.

"Thank you both for stepping outside," you begin. "I have a responsibility to get back to my class as soon as possible. Conor, your behavior is not meeting the expectations I have of all of my students in my classroom." You breathe. Wait for the defensive interruption either from the mother or from Conor. In your head, your Zen Master voice speaks over their raucous tones, "Don't engage. Don't engage. Don't engage."

You pretend to listen to their defensiveness and wait for your opening. "I hear that you don't agree with me," you respond. "The central issue is that for you to reenter my classroom, Conor, you will need to follow the directions I went over at the beginning of the class." You repeat the expectations for the benefit of both Conor and his mother. "I am going back into my classroom," you say. "I would like for you to join me. Would you like to come back in with me?"

You know that for a limit-setting conference to be effective, you need to provide two options, both of which you are comfortable with, and then let the child choose. This helps foster the child's ownership of the outcome of the conversation.

The subtleties of what you just did cannot be overstated. In no way did you chastise the mother. It is not your job to be the judge and jury of adults. It is your job to help children develop socially and academically. You did not argue or negotiate. You did not get caught up on the social drama or lose sight of your mission to get back to your other students promptly. If the child decides to stay outside—which is a very distinct option—his mother is with him. Quite possibly, the mother will lash out at Conor because she is embarrassed. Unless the child is in danger, you need to stay out of that.

Involving parents can be tricky, especially when you have to run a classroom, which quite often feels like herding cats.

➔ WHAT TACTIC WILL YOU TRY NEXT?—P. 107

Option 6. Handle Parents Who Have a Fight in Your Classroom

YOU thought you detected some snippiness between two parents helping in your classroom, but you shrugged it off. You thought you had imagined it. It turns out you had not. Later, you try to recount the warning signs. You faintly remember two subtleties that you overlooked: one of the parents was uncharacteristically quiet, withdrawn, and physically removed from the other parents. When that first parent tried to share an idea, another parent showed typical negative body language—eyes rolling, arms folded, and head shaking.

Now the yelling has begun. You quickly convince the two warring parents to step out of the room. Your first reaction is to ask them to go to the main office to discuss their problem or, better yet, leave campus.

You stop before doing that, though, because you think you might be able to mediate the problem. If you are unsuccessful, you can ask someone in the front office to come down and escort the parents off campus. However, the clock is ticking, and you need to get back to your students.

You ask a neighboring teacher to watch your class while you stand in the hallway for the three minutes it will take to settle this misunderstanding. You already know from working with students that the root of the most drama on campus is misunderstanding.

You stand where you can see both parents. There is about two feet separating the combatants. You can still see their clenched teeth and knuckles. Your first priority is to get their commitment to resolve the problem. You find yourself talking to them in the same manner you would talk to students who have acted out.

"Thank you for coming outside with me. That behavior outburst is not welcome in my classroom. For you to be welcome back into my classroom, you two need to figure this out. I can help you, but I have a responsibility to be back with my students. I can give you three minutes, if you want my help."

What you said was crucial on many fronts:

You started off with a "Thank you."

You talked directly to them and set specific limits: "That behavior outburst is not welcome in my classroom."

You set a goal for the parents: "For you to be welcome back into my classroom, you two need to figure this out."

You offered your help, being mindful of time restrictions and your responsibilities, "I can help you, but I have a responsibility to be back with my students. I can give you three minutes, if you want my help."

Most probably, one of four things will happen (in order of probability):

1. One parent or both will abandon the scene and go home, or
2. The parents will shrug off their embarrassment, mumble apologies, and re-enter your classroom, or
3. The problem will escalate and you will need to call people from the main office down to your classroom, or
4. They may ask for your help.

In the ten seconds it takes for both parents to breathe, collect themselves, and agree to be heard, you recall a website you came across in college. Apparently Canadian farmers needed help mediating disputes, so the Ontario Ministry of Agriculture offered some key points for conflict resolution

(Ontario Ministry of Agriculture, Food and Rural Affairs, 2006). You now use what you read there to help these parents find common ground.

What is essential is that the parents feel heard. Behind most conflicts is a breakdown in communication. Maintaining equilibrium and a calm demeanor are the key elements of your success in dealing with this problem.

The parents tell you that they want you to help them. You turn to them and set the ground rules: "Both of you will be heard. I will hear one voice at a time. Do you agree to this?"

Checking in for consent throughout the process is important to conflict management. After you hear—uninterrupted—from the first parent, you turn to the second parent to check for understanding. "Thank you for not interrupting. What did you hear?"

After the second parent talks, you say to the first, "Thank you for not interrupting. What did you hear?"

"It is obvious that both of you are hurt. What do you need to be able to move forward? Once again, I need to hear one voice at a time."

Before the parents have the privilege of returning to your classroom, it is vital that you reset your expectations: "I really respect your ability to move forward. Your outburst is still vivid in the minds of the students. Please wait on your need to talk about this further until you leave my classroom. Our collective unwavering mission is to focus on the students right now."

→ WHAT TACTIC WILL YOU TRY NEXT?—P. 107

11. Field Trips

Planning a Field Trip: Getting Buy-in from All Involved Parties

BECAUSE the end goal of schooling is preparing students for the "real world," you decide to take them out into the real world. Your first thought is to go somewhere fun—the movies, an amusement park, bowling, something that will be unforgettable. After daydreaming, you come to realize that you will need to sell your idea to get any traction. That means you will need to sell it to:

1. The principal, who will need to trust you with students and the school's reputation.
2. Your colleagues, who will feel the impact of students who will be staying behind.
3. The broader community, who will have to support your idea of providing less overtly structured academic preparedness time.
4. The students, who will either make the trip a pleasure or a nightmare.

After thinking it over and talking with your principal, you realize your trip has to be standards-based. This is much easier to accomplish than you thought initially. Academic standards are written to be malleable. You are the academic expert. Once you get back from the trip, students can write reflective essays to meet that requirement. Now you need buy-in from all involved parties.

Students: You have never met a student who didn't want to go on a field trip. You have met several students who, for malicious reasons or through true obliviousness, managed to mess up your field trip. Conversely, the vast majority of students will cherish the opportunities you give them. Throughout the entire field-trip process, you are a role model. By organizing and implementing field trips, you broaden students' view of what is possible in life. The ones who earn the trip thrive from new firsthand experiences in the real world. The students who do not earn the trip get the message to improve their work ethic and behavior. Accountability is key.

Parents: Your goal is to have parents breathe a sigh of relief on the first day of school when they see your name on their child's class schedule. Parents initially seek collaboration with their children's teachers. Unfortunately, no matter what you do, you will always come up short against many parents' unrealistic expectations. This disappointment is magnified for the parents of children who have not earned the privilege of joining a field trip. By organizing field trips, you can be a role model for parents and students alike to reach for more. Through field trips, you can position yourself as someone who brings out the best in students by bringing them more opportunities to thrive.

Administrators: Beyond just ensuring the safety of all children, you carry the banner of your school's reputation when you go on a field trip. When you follow through on a successful field trip, your administrators will learn that you are trustworthy and dependable. By demonstrating your reliability on a field trip, you will earn new freedom in your classroom.

Colleagues: If you do field trips well, you may alienate your colleagues. Students will miss other classes and then come back possibly too excited to do any work. Also, you will need your colleagues to either come with you to chaperone or cover classes back at school for you. Remember that field trips are a team effort. Stay humble and respect your colleagues' concerns to keep them on board with any plans you make for a field trip. Any attempt to set up field trips for self-glorification will backfire, but any attempt to set up field trips to better students' lives will be honored.

Community: Ultimately, we are all judged by our actions, and being the person who creates field trip opportunities for students may bring some risk. However, from the community point of view, your value skyrockets when you have the courage to respectfully reach out to the community and embrace the risk of going on a field trip.

Before you go on any field trip, you need to figure out which academic standards the trip will address and the student qualifications for going on the trip. One of the most important parts of planning, though, is funding for any trip.

Funding a Field Trip

You may be lucky enough to have money in your classroom budget to take your students on a field trip this year. If not, you have found several other options for funding field trips:

1. You can take up a collection from the families you serve. It is simple to send an e-mail home asking that parents pay for this trip. This may spur parents to be very engaged in students' progress in earning the trip. If a child earns the trip but the family can't contribute, you can arrange with the student to work in your classroom to earn the money for the trip. You'll have to have another option available for students and families who simply can't pay to go on the trip. And you will need to keep accurate records of payments so you can refund them if you need to, such as when a family has paid but their child hasn't earned the trip.

2. The goal of the PTA is to fund projects and resources for student opportunities. To apply for a PTA grant, you will need to prepare a presentation of how the field trip is essential for your standards-based academic goals. A great way to ensure PTA support is to offer to bring in students to give a debriefing presentation of what they learned from the field trip. Chances are, they will not want to fund your entire trip. If you have already done some informal fundraising by soliciting donations from companies or discounts at the site of the field trip, share that with your PTA.

3. You can apply for a grant from an outside agency. To find such an agency, you can search the Internet using the key words, "classroom field trip grants," which will yield more than a million results. Supporting schools is great public relations for hundreds of companies and foundations. The money is out there. Writing a grant application is like writing an essay for any other type of application. The questions on any grant application fall into several categories: (1) demographics of your school, (2) field trip agenda, (3) academic standards the field trip will address, (4) reasons why the field trip is essential to your academic program, and (5) costs for your field trip. You should ask a colleague to read what you've written, and then you need to make sure you don't miss the due dates for the grant. You can probably use your essay for more than one application. If you do receive monies from outside agencies, you should always write a thank you letter! It is best if you do not rely on a single funding source but instead create a hybrid of revenue sources.

How do you choose to handle field-trips, both their preparation and eventualities? You:

Following is a discussion of each option. You can move from one to the next, or you can jump between options at any time.

Option 1. Create Positive Behavior Expectations for the Field Trip

YOU are planning a field trip for next week. You know that you have a better chance of the trip going well if you tell students what to expect and what you expect from them:

"Congratulations," you start out, "I am so thrilled that you have earned the trip next week. Just so there are no mysteries or confusion, we will take ten minutes now and collectively brainstorm your expectations for the trip.

"My goal is for you to be personally responsible for this trip. What that means is that I want you to come up with your behavioral expectations for the trip and consequences. The more personal ownership you have in your adventure, the more you will grow and appreciate this trip. Please pair off and come up with what you think the behavioral standards should be for students on this trip."

With the constant time pressure that is built into the amount of work any teacher needs to cover in one school year, having students invest ten minutes for this discussion may seem like a waste of time. The reality is that you are saving time. People naturally abide more by rules they have participated in formulating. When students are part of any process, they value the product more.

While students share their ideas, you model non-critical brainstorming. On your front board, you write as they talk. This process takes no more than five minutes. When all of the ideas are on the board, you ask, "Do you see any common themes?" Students see related themes come up over and over again. You draw lines connecting comments to one another, until you come up with the push to find one central theme.

"Is there any way we can combine these three leftover concepts into one rule?" The wording may vary in enumerable ways, but essentially, that one student-generated rule will most likely be something like "Think beyond yourself" or "Respect yourself, other people, and your surroundings."

To close off the expectation discussion, you need a carrot and stick: "Obviously, this is a privilege to go on this trip. I'm thrilled that you made the choice to earn it.

"Your discussion in class today is your warning. If you decide to act in any way that embarrasses yourself, your family, our school, or our community, you will lose all privileges on the field trip and I will make arrangements to send you home as soon as possible. All school rules of highest social respect will be in effect during the entire trip, including during the bus ride.

"In all honesty, this trip is not about you. Your behavior enables me to set up more field trips in the future. You are obligated to do your best on this trip so that other students can go on field trips in the future. This is a team effort."

On the day of the trip, you remind students about this talk before leaving campus: "The field trip starts now. If you think you will be tempted to do anything that may undermine our team's day, please go back to the main office now. If you decide to stay with us, I will be thrilled. I know you will make smart choices throughout our day together." You always make give students a way out and end on a positive note. Students will rise to your expectations.

When you think about this approach, you see that there are several key resonating benefits. Students find themselves to be critical to the process. Their voices are heard. They usually have higher standards than adults do. In students' minds, they remember all of their rules. You, on the other hand, only have to remember one rule. You can follow through on countless situations under this one umbrella. So when something goes wrong, and something will go wrong, you can cite the one rule that will cover any event.

Once you are on the trip, you see two students begin shoving each other playfully. Their behavior screams out that more trouble is coming. All you need to do is walk over, make eye contact, and ask, "Are you respecting each other? Are you following your own class's expectations?"

Even though you threatened to send students home, that should be your last option. Students will respect you more if you hold them accountable in a consistent manner but also offer second chances.

→ How do you handle things next?—p. 118

Option 2. You Set Up the Perfect Trip

JUST like every other element of your work, planning, focus, and follow-through are the main ingredients for success. After soliciting input from veteran colleagues, you map out your own field trip. After many personal attempts, observations, and discussions, you start to have a sense of the critical factors in setting up a perfect trip.

Pre-planning: Just like anything worthwhile, you need to start to plan for this trip weeks, if not months ahead of time.

Mapping out behavioral expectations: You will make your trip invitation-only. What this means is that given enough notice, students should earn the trip with exemplary behavior and passing grades. Your goal is to get everyone on the bus. Having the caveat that students need to earn everything in life enables you a way to leave your most troublesome students behind. Unfortunately, these are quite often the same students who need the trip the most. While your soul may want to include your wayward, potentially trouble-seeking students on the trip, your brain must override this urge. Your school trip will be a public example of your school's behavioral expectations. Allowing all students to be on the bus without earning it opens the floodgates of problems you will have to deal with on the road.

To set your behavioral expectations, you will need to be clear about how you expect students to behave. Don't fall for the fallacy that students will "step up" their behavior during a field trip. The illusion of freedom on a field trip exacerbates old problems and negative behavior habits at school.

On page 121 is a tool[4] that lists behavior expectations so students can see their progress. Ideally, you start this process six weeks before the field trip so there aren't any last-minute surprises of who will be attending and who hasn't earned the privilege of going.

To begin, you give each student a piece of paper like the one on page 121. The paper is printed on both sides with the same list of the characteristics you would like students to model to represent the school well. On one side, students evaluate themselves; on the other side, you evaluate the student. The bottom of the paper offers room for comments from you, the student, or parents. In essence, this form is the paper trail you need in order to justify bringing any child on the trip. To earn a trip, a student must earn a 3 in each category. It is *imperative* that you allow each child to hope that he or she can earn the trip; you do this by, as educator Eric Kruger says, "catching them doing things right."

In Week One, students work on their side of the page first, writing 1, 2, or 3 for each characteristic listed. The paper then comes to you, the teacher. On your side of the paper, for each characteristic, you write a 3 if the student reliably demonstrates that skill, a 2 if the student is inconsistent in showing the characteristic, or a 1 if the student isn't making any positive progress in dependability for that category. You then write any pertinent comments at the bottom of the paper. Naturally, students ask if a 3 can ever fall to a 2. "Your goal is to continue doing your best work so you don't fall to a 2," you answer.

---

4 This, along with much of the philosophy that informs this book, is an adaptation of what I learned through working with my primary mentor and teaching colleague, Eric Kruger. I worked with Eric between 1997 and 2007, and while no written account of his pedagogical practices exists, I hope to give due credit to the source of so many excellent ideas.

Behavior Expectations

Characteristics	Week				
	1	2	3	4	Final
Respects adults					
Respects other students					
Responsible—comes prepared					
Integrity—is trustworthy (not sneaky)					
Patience—good self-control without being told					
Invests in Community—uses good judgment					
Initiative—takes action to own education					
Cooperation in group activities					
Reliability—follows through and does homework					
Punctuality—attendance/is on time					
Maturity—not a whiner					
Persistence—puts forth sincere effort					
Follows directions					
Shows leadership					

Based on the above and your judgment, please select the category below that best ranks this student.

Definitely *should* participate					
Possibly should participate					
Probably should not participate					
Definitely *should not* participate					

Scoring

- ► 3 = Responsible
- ► 2 = Sometimes
- ► 1 = Needs major improvement

The next day, you hand the forms back to each student. Students then take the forms home for parents' signatures to make sure that everyone understands the process and the specific categories for growth. Students bring the forms back to you the next day. Obviously, many of these sheets will be lost or abandoned by the student in transit. That is why there are the "Follows Directions" and "Integrity" listings. A conscientious teacher has replacement copies readily available.

This back-and-forth process continues for a month. Your knowledge and awareness of each student's maturation and efforts toward growth are put to the test. It is incumbent on you to personalize the form and note positive growth in specific categories.

This process is much more expedient than it appears. For the first week, there is a major time investment—about one to two minutes per student. For a normal middle- or high-school class load of 180 students, this can equal a six-hour expenditure of time. The payoff of high expectations far surpasses this outlay of time. Once students have clarity of purpose, this motivates them to elevate their work habits and social interactions. It is a good idea to schedule field trips right before state testing, so students power into the high point of their work year with a rigorous month of high expectations.

Your expectations will never go lower, and students will rise to meet them. Starting in the third week, you start to hand out field trip permission forms to students who have consistently earned 3s throughout the process. If time permits in the instructional schedule, your best move as a role model is to call up each invited student, one at a time. Ideally, you say a few words about each student that you call up. This is a special moment for the entire class. Students will seek the public recognition of doing things right. Merely handing out the field trip forms is anti-climactic.

By the end of the fourth week, if you have done your job right, 99 percent of the students have earned the trip. For the few noncompliant students, you have the time to conduct individual quick conferences and outline specific behaviors each needs to demonstrate to earn a seat on the bus.

You remind students who have secured a seat on the bus that invitations can be revoked even on the day of the trip. They must maintain their exemplary work to come along. Ripping up a student's invitation is an exceptionally rare event. You do not lose sight that the goal is to make this trip inviting to all students and hopefully, to get all students on the bus.

As for the few students who choose with their actions not to join the trip, you farm them out to other classrooms. You provide a stack of work for these students to complete. Your expectation of academic rigor never falters. Even for these students, you try to maintain a sense of hope for them by planning multiple opportunities during the course of the year for each to aspire to earn.

Free and reduced lunches: You know that your school's cafeteria services are mandated to provide lunches for qualified students whether they are at school or on a field trip. You touch base with cafeteria workers to make arrangements for your students who qualify, and you give them a courteous thank you and some flowers to show appreciation for their extra effort. On the day of the trip, you will pack some additional lunches for students who might have left their lunches at home.

Delegate: Not everything needs to be on your shoulders. More people want to help you than you know of. You think about the big picture of the trip and then look through your plans so far. You don't want to be mired in minutiae. What can you put in someone else's hands to do for you? You know that you want to keep some details in your own hands. A week before the trip, you check on the bus. Throughout the planning, you keep track of the money. When you do delegate, you need to have faith that people will follow through, but you can always double-check anything that volunteers do for you.

Implementation/The day of the trip: During the planning phase, you sit down and create a list of the things you think of as a must for the day of the trip:

- Student downtime and time to socialize
- Reflection on the purpose of the trip
- Mementos of the trip (Quite often, these will be donated by the field trip site; it never hurts to ask).
- Relevance to the larger meaning behind your curriculum (Look for broader purposes, such as "community involvement," "environmental stewardship," and so on).
- Fun.
- Challenge and growth for students to see the world in a new way.
- Low expense.
- Food (Pack emergency food in case a kid forgets lunch).
- Emergency plan (Follow your school's protocol for responding to emergencies).
- Forgiveness for all of the participants on the trip in case they misbehave.
- Patience.
- Support for parental volunteers.
- Flexibility (You will need to model this for all of the participants).
- Accessibility for all students.
- Age appropriateness.
- Student input.

What to take along: You have been advised by a veteran teacher to prepare a detailed script (with flex time included), along with contact phone numbers to hand out to each parent volunteer and administrative staff member. You remember that you will want to bring a first aid kit and the students' permission slips, which should list health conditions, so you are ready for an emergency.

While you are on the trip: Once students are on the bus, you issue a reminder about your behavioral expectations. You make time to check in with parent chaperones periodically. This simple action will tell parents that you don't take them for granted and that you are fully responsible throughout the day. You remind yourself that this is your trip and your responsibility. If any emergency arises, you are as prepared as you can be. You vow to remain composed. If you freak out, students will freak out, and all is lost. The calmer you are, the calmer everyone else around you will be.

Follow-up: Once everyone is back at school safe and sound, you have students write thank-you notes for the field trip site and all donors and volunteers who helped with the trip. You remind them to make each letter only three paragraphs long: The first paragraph is about what happened on the trip. In the second paragraph, the student makes connections between the events on the trip and the academic content they are learning in class. In the third paragraph, the student writes about what the addressee did to make the trip possible, whether it was financial help, being a docent or chaperone, or any other contribution.

A well-run field trip is where your teaching legend is born.

→ HOW DO YOU HANDLE THINGS NEXT?—P. 118

Option 3. You Lose a Student

YOU and your students are on a field trip at a local bakery. You have been diligent about taking attendance. Now you think Sophia is missing. You take roll again. Sophia *is* missing!

What do you do now? Do you go public with your anxiety? If you do go public, whom do you tell? Parent chaperones? Chaperones and students? Can you ask the people who work at the bakery for help? Because you still have a responsibility to the entire group, how can you move forward? The rest of the students are still entitled to enjoy the field trip.

Your first thought is, obviously, that you want all of your students to be safe.

Breathe. Now you feel a little calmer. You decide that you *will not* leave the scene and you *will* ask for help. The next step is to call school to cover yourself, but you also need to stand your ground in doing what is right for the situation right now. You are ultimately responsible for the well-being of all of the people under your watch.

"When is the last time anyone saw Sophia?" you ask the group.

People are shocked. You can hear a few mumbles of exasperation.

You decide you need to set the tone. "I need to see your eyes right now!" you say with authority. "This is a team effort. Accidents happen. If you wish to spend your energy being negative stay here and don't help. If you want to be part of the solution, I need you with me right now."

The overwhelming majority of students flock to your side. Predictably, the two to three students who barely made the trip because of behavior issues defiantly stay put. You ask a parent chaperone to supervise those students.

You know that students of all ages, regardless of what they say or their pretense at being cool, want to help; they want to know that adults rely on them. You ask chaperones to stand with the students that offered to help. You have as many search groups as you do chaperones. Your recalcitrant non-searchers can function as the home base.

"Most important, everyone stay together," you caution. "We are not going to lose more students. We need to retrace our steps since the last time I took roll. No matter what happens, everyone return here in ten minutes." This is when you assign scouting groups to various sectors from your field trip. You remember a colleague's advice to rely on the people who work at the site of your field trip.

You now call the school. Ultimately, you need to model the importance of having faith that things do work out for the best. The truth will always come out.

If she is not found, you can stay; just because the buses need to leave does not mean you have to. You know that you *will not* leave until you find Sophia. One of the parent chaperones can act as bus monitor. Your ultimate priority is the safety of all of your students.

When Sophia is finally found, your work begins. The students who have found her want to be seen as gallant heroes. Sophia is shaken and deeply embarrassed. You first call the school to tell them that you have Sophia. You need to control the narrative of how this incident is seen by others. If you were negligent in your supervision duties, you will need to own that mistake. The quicker you come clean, the quicker the problem will go away. If the mistake was Sophia's, you will need to rise above any finger pointing and model the forgiveness you would want for yourself.

You next take thirty seconds to help the "hero children" frame their stories. "Great job," you say to the heroes. "Thank you for your help. But don't forget this was a team effort. Every student helped in one way or another. What is more important than you finding Sophia is that everyone is safe. Thank you for being part of the process." And you leave it at that.

Now for Sophia. Your time with her needs to be supportive and listening. Any punitive yelling at her will only decimate this child. You will have time later to reinforce your expectations. Sophia needs you to be supportive and kind right now. She will need some time with her friends. You try to keep from hovering over her. More than anything, she will need to be treated like any other child.

Once you get back to campus, you stay with Sophia until her parents arrive. You explain what happened, and the parent greatly appreciates your candor. You know that the more you try to cover up the incident—especially at this early stage, when no one knows how Sophia became lost—the more imperiled you will be later. Throughout the discussion, keep your focus on the emotional and physical safety of Sophia.

Dealing with a lost child is draining for everyone involved. Your cool temperament will keep everyone involved calm.

→ HOW DO YOU HANDLE THINGS NEXT?—P. 118

Option 4. Improvise Around Last-Minute Surprises

YOU and your class have finally left on a field trip you started planning months ago. You believe you have covered all of your bases to make this day go smoothly. You called ahead. You walked through the trip the week before. Your bus has arrived at the site on time. You get all of your students off of the bus and you take roll again.

That's when you hit your first bump. As your contact at the site of the field trip approaches you, he says, "I'm sorry to tell you, but our main attraction is closed." Your mouth falls open.

"We're terribly sorry," he repeats. Sorry? *Sorry*? You have a busload of students and nothing to do with them. Your months of thorough preparation and planning have just gone out the window.

Wait a minute, you tell yourself. Breathe. There is always a solution. Maybe you can still make this work.

"I'll be right back," you say to him. You go to one of your parental chaperones and ask her to have the students take out their notebooks with a worksheet you had handed out in the bus. An essential part of any field trip is observation. Students will now list and describe, on the worksheet, ten sensory details for each of their five senses. By having students work on their sensory map, you are freed up to make new plan. You have probably bought yourself ten minutes.

You immediately think, "What do I do now?" You think back to a mentor's various pieces of advice:

1. Don't lose sight of your academic standards. Why are you on this trip? Which curricular standards are you aiming for? What is your core mission?
2. Crowd control. Don't let on to students that you are ever out of control. If you must, fake it. Stay on course for your end goal. Everything will work out if you keep your cool.
3. Time frame. You still have time commitments during your trip. The bus is still scheduled to take you back to campus. You may have to fill in some open time. Ultimately, students would rather do team-building exercises during a field trip than in a classroom.
4. Breathe. The calmer you are, the more control you have. Stay professional. You need to model for students how to roll with what life throws at you.

While students are still in your sight filling in their sensory worksheets, you return to your field trip contact. "What do you propose we do now that the reason we are here is no longer accessible?" This conversation can go in one of two directions, but ultimately both paths connect to one trail. (1) Either your docent will offer suggestions and you two will brainstorm a solution together, or (2) He throws up a roadblock, shrugs his shoulders, and offers no help. If you do have to make the plan yourself, you'll be able to do so; you walked this field trip last week.

Clock is ticking. Some students are already finished with their worksheet. You ask them to coach other students while you gather your chaperones to solidify your augmented plan. You tell the chaperones what has happened and what you plan to do about it; your sense of calm and directedness is instantly contagious. You find you have a broad range of support.

What ultimately saves you is a list of cooperative games you stashed in your backpack for moments like this. During your transition, you find yourself filling in small blocks of time with team-building games. You found some ideas on the Internet. By typing in the key words "team building games," you found half a trillion options.

After you return to school, your resiliency and composure is what students and parents end up remembering most of the trip.

→ HOW DO YOU HANDLE THINGS NEXT?—P. 118

Option 5. Deal with Buses that are Late or Broken Down

YOU are in the middle of planning another field trip, but you keep thinking about the last one you took with students. It all worked out, but you want your next one to be drama-free.

You are now checking and double-checking all details. You know that the more prepared you are, the more easily you can adapt to any surprises. Then, on the morning of your trip, you learn that there is a problem with the bus you had arranged. It's not clear whether the bus will be late or just not show up. The secretary in the front office, who told you the bad news, seems to be as perplexed as you are.

So what do you do? Many of your parent chaperones have made special child care accommodations for their children who are not in your class. Your students want to go on a trip *now*. You are afraid you won't be able to deliver.

Breathe. First, you need to bring your principal up to date. "I know you are busy and I'm sorry for interrupting you," you say, "but I need to keep you up to date on today's field trip. We don't know the status of the buses. I have several parents and all of my students who are anxiously waiting to know what to do."

Even though it is your principal's job to put out fires, it doesn't mean you can't help be a part of the fire brigade. You hand him a bucket of solutions:

"I want to bring them all in my classroom and do team-building activities. Is it okay if I go ahead with this plan for the next thirty minutes, until we hear from the bus company if they will be sending buses or not? If they do send buses—great, we'll just go the trip late. If they don't send buses, I would like to my students to just re-join their regular school day. If we go on this trip this morning—great. If we need to cancel the trip or reschedule it, I will follow through."

You are very mindful of what you just presented. You are not overreacting. You have your backup plan, and you are able to adjust to any outcome. Most of all, you have alleviated the need for your principal to solve the problem.

After the principal agrees to your plan, you talk with the parent volunteers. You radiate the confidence and flexibility you would like to see everyone follow. You find that parents are much more amenable to having a day off than you would think. They are absolved from going on the field trip and they have child care for the day. One of your potential problems will be to bring the parents back if you need to reschedule the field trip.

If you do need to postpone the trip, you need to make sure the lunches are not wasted. Students still need to eat.

Your year is not this one field trip. Your year is the composure, professionalism, and responsible role modeling you do every day.

→ HOW DO YOU HANDLE THINGS NEXT?—P. 118

Option 6. Mediate a Parent Complaint

TODAY'S trip is humming along. Your plans have come together and all seems well. While the students are engaged in one part of the trip, you have a moment to check in with your parent chaperones. "How are things going so far?" you ask.

"I have never been more disappointed in how a teacher has treated my daughter," says this mother. "And consequently, so far this has been a lost year for my daughter."

Your head tilts forward and your mouth falls open. Where is this deluge of venom coming from? You were just checking in about the field trip. How long has this parent wanted to bring up her concerns? Why now at the field trip? Is the kid really having a "lost year?" You immediately think back to her daughter's performance in your classroom. Yeah, her daughter isn't perfect—but lost? No.

You are torn between wanting to know how legitimate her concerns are and trying to get back to managing the field trip. You decide to give this parent another minute to see if you can get more information.

"Wow, I had no idea you felt that way," you begin. "My priority at this moment is keeping this field trip going, but I have five minutes to talk with you right now. I'm always interested in improving my practice so I can meet my students' needs. Can you tell me specific examples of what I've done in my classroom that leads you to feel that way?"

You are ready to listen politely if the parent cites some specifics. You will not make excuses, because it is useless to argue about past events. You are always willing to listen to input that helps you improve your teaching practices.

However, this particular parent hems and haws and then says, "I can't tell you a specific example. It is just a feeling I have. My daughter could be doing more." The parent's motivation becomes clear. She is trying to get under your skin because of her own issues. This conversation really has nothing to do with you. Because the parent's concerns aren't really about you, you stay out of it.

Ultimately the best response is, "Thank you for being open with me. The more you communicate your concerns, the better I can help all students." And walk away.

→ HOW DO YOU HANDLE THINGS NEXT?—P. 118

Option 7. Deal with a Purchase Order that is for the Wrong Amount

AS the students step off the bus, you walk over to your contact at the site of the field trip to complete last-minute paperwork. You are caught by surprise when you hand over the district purchase order and your field trip contact rejects it.

"I'm sorry, but this purchase order has not been written for a large enough amount to pay for this event. Your students cannot enter."

Breathe and remain calm. "I have a busload of students," you say. "We are completing this field trip today. Either you are helping me or I am going to work with your manager. What solutions can you offer?"

You remember that the fine print of any purchase order stipulates a 10 percent margin of error. Even if the purchase order is for less than what you need, you have wiggle room.

Stand your ground. Your focus needs to be on seeing this field trip through. You can deal with any of the monetary fallout once you get back to campus.

➜ HOW DO YOU HANDLE THINGS NEXT?—P. 118

12. Organizing a School Club

ONE small step at a time—this is the mantra you tried to adopt coming out of your credential program. Through the deluge of being a new teacher you have had to keep multiple balls up in the air simultaneously:

- ▸ Curriculum
- ▸ Classroom Management
- ▸ Collegiality
- ▸ Classroom outreach to parents
- ▸ Courteous relationship with the administration

While the five High C's may seem like a short list, you are experiencing the multitude of layers—both obvious and hidden—within each category. Throughout your life, you have realized that taking small bites and savoring each new mouthful aides digestion while avoiding indigestion; the last thing you want to do is bite off more than you can chew. At least, that was your intent until you spent a lunch period out in the schoolyard.

It is late March. You have found your footing. You have even been able to plan ahead in your curriculum, and on the whole, you are feeling more and more confident every day. As a semi-reward for your diligence, you decide not to work during this lunch period.

The fresh air is just that—refreshing after a stormy winter. The cacophony of "Hi's and "What are you doing out here?" is fairly intense for the first five minutes. Then, almost as quickly as you became the focus of attention, students seem to look past you, re-engaging in their own worlds. Lunchtime is the most intense time of day for most students. Managing social interaction requires a completely different skill-set than do most academic content areas—and is often more rigorous.

School stress is a well-documented factor of student life. With the onslaught of bully-awareness, the hidden, non-academic life of our youth is under more and more national scrutiny. You think back to your own high school experience and you remember one recommended fix—"Mix It Up Day." You sit down in the middle of the lunch area, take out your phone, and quickly look up the Teaching Tolerance website.

"In our surveys, students have identified the cafeteria as the place where divisions are most clearly drawn. So on one day—October 30 this school year—we ask students to move out of their comfort zones and connect with someone new over lunch. It's a simple act with profound implications. Studies have shown that interactions across group lines can help reduce prejudice. When students interact with those who are different from them, biases and misperceptions can fall away."

At first you hesitate. You are still relatively new to the profession and the last thing you want to do is cause school-wide seismic shake with new plans and ideas. But your school needs something.

The cliques and niches into which students segregate themselves are obvious and natural. With the information overload that is the norm for students, wanting to spend downtime with a few trusted friends is logical. Intermixed within these groves of laughing friends, the students who sit alone as solitary saplings are hard to ignore.

You start to think about the stress in students' young lives. Would a lunchtime club help? What would the club do? How much effort would it take to start a club? How can you maintain your own balance? Can you start something new and still not be overwhelmed with your already growing list of responsibilities? What does the school need?

You sit and watch. It needs something. You remember back to your credential work, specifically Stephen Krashen's influence on language acquisition. "Learners with a low affective filter will not only be efficient language acquirers of the comprehensible input they receive. They are also more likely to interact with others, unembarrassed by making mistakes for example, and thus increase the amount of that input." (Krashen 2003) In other words, the more comfortable students are in the school world, the better they will perform, grow, and flourish.

Morally and ethically, it is imperative to provide as much support as one can to help kids thrive. But when you realize that prominent pedagogical thinkers support your stance, you feel even more enthused than before. If you could provide some solace for students' school angst, you can become part of your school's engine geared towards improved academic performance.

Obviously, there are as many clubs as there are hobbies and social causes in the world. Not withstanding the content of your school club concept, you already know that everything in life needs to be managed well to succeed. Minor Myers, Jr.'s quote comes to mind: "Go into the world and do well. More importantly, go into the world and do good." That is exactly what you want to do—some good. The focus of your club will morph, develop, and grow.

The first thing you need to do is get administrative approval. You will need to follow your school's protocol for authorization. Once your idea has received a firm endorsement, then you can begin selling the idea to students. You could promote your club through the school newsletter, the morning announcements, and the school website. Most of all, you can promote it in the hallway. Ideally, your core of founding students should also promote the club. If you'r seeking a specific type of student, reach out to them in the hallway. Throughout this time, you will be promoting one consistent message—a blurb about the goal of your club, when it is meeting, and where.

You brace yourself for this new adventure. The process your club will go through and obstacles it will overcome during the group's maturation are fairly predictable.

How do you manage your club to provide opportunities for students to thrive? You:

Following is a discussion of each option. You can move from one to the next, or you can jump between options at any time.

Option 1. Students Dismiss Your Club Idea as a Gathering of Losers

YOUR plan seems golden at the start. Standing in the hallway during passing periods, you see your share of questionable behavior. To the casual observer, students are just being students, jostling in the hallways, laughing, and being loud. Because you are a more careful observer, you see students getting shoved, getting laughed at, and being excluded. You decide your club needs to be a safe haven for targets, for students who have nowhere else to go. To get to know your intended club members better, you do some research. You are astonished to find that there are about 2.7 million students being bullied each year—by about 2.1 million other students. Make Beats, Not Beat Downs, an anti-bullying website, cites this and other eye-opening statistics:

- One in 7 students in Grades K–12 is either a bully or has been a victim of bullying.
- 56 percent of students have personally witnessed some type of bullying at school.
- 15 percent of all school absenteeism is directly related to fears of being bullied at school.
- 1 out of every 10 students who drops out of school does so because of repeated bullying.
- 90 percent of 4th through 8th graders report being victims of bullying.

Your mind is made up. You can, you must, and you will do something to help. You decide to start off with small steps. Logically, if bullying is a contributing factor for absenteeism, and Mondays are quite often the day when students are absent, you will host your Safe Haven Club on Mondays. You want students to come to school, and if this club can be a hook, you are all in. You decide you would like to let students decide what to do once they show up for the club. Getting students in the door is your main objective.

For the first few weeks, you are thrilled with the turnout. Twenty or thirty students show up weekly for the first month. Unfortunately, very few of the students are return visitors. Your numbers start to dwindle after the fourth week, so you examine what's behind your shifting enrollment.

Students aren't committed to your idea. Voyeuristically, they are just checking out the scene. You think back to one of your under division introduction to sociology classes, and you remember Erving Goffman's work about "social stigmas." Have you set up a group intended to welcome in students only to have them be labeled as social deviants or targets? You feel like an idiot. No wonder your group never developed a stable student base of interested students. Your club idea is uncool.

It is more and more obvious to you. The students have dismissed your club idea as a gathering of losers. This explains the superficial voyeurism. No one wants to be labeled as a member of your group, but everyone is interested in who shows up. You shudder to think of how you may have inadvertently caused some students to be more ostracized than ever before.

So the problem remains. How can you develop a club that gives students a safe social place to be? Most important, how can you create a club where students want to be?

How can you develop cool?

You recently read Malcolm Gladwell's *Tipping Point* analysis of the elements involved in creating a social epidemic. The major concept that now leaps out at you from his work is the importance of social connectors, context, and content. Your club's participants matter as much as the content.

When your club has substance and a healthy mix of people, you are more confident than ever you can make this idea fly.

Your "to do" list becomes clear. You need to be the connector. Everyone can develop social capital. You decide to spend your time becoming a social capital investment banker. Your portfolio of assets rises when you connect with students in the hallway; are available to open jammed lockers; are a wellspring of encouragement; hold students accountable when they mess up; and, most of all, when you are aware of your students' emotional needs.

The content of your club still matters. The value of your club is directly dependent on how much good it does. In addition to the service element of your club, the more you are attuned and open to the subtleties of your students' needs, the more students will want to invest in your club, and the less alien your club will be. The less alien your club seems, the less its members will be considered outliers.

The social calculus of generalized reciprocity is real. You don't want anyone to be indebted to you. You decide to think of this as a karma issue; the more you do for other people the more credence your club will gain.

➔ WHAT STRATEGY WILL YOU TRY NEXT?—P. 130

Option 2. Solicit a Co-Founder and Navigate Success

A MONTH after you start your club, you begin to wonder if you should worry about fire-code violations. It looks like your social investment is starting to pay off — how many students can fit in one classroom anyway? You don't want to offend anyone by turning people away, but you are only one person.

You realize that the more additional staff members you include, the stronger your school club will be. The benefits of inclusivity are numerous. We all get locked into our own worlds. Opening up your work to collaboration brings along the benefit of perspective. In the ongoing drive to improvement, having multiple points of view as to your club's effectiveness and shortcomings can only contribute to the quality of the end product.

You start to unpack why you think collaboration is worth the investment. Above all, it helps kids. For people who see teaching as more than just a job, but as a responsibility to nurture community building and self-development, teaming fulfills deeper purposes. Teaming enables teachers to diversify their skill sets. Communication skills and empathy development flourish when teachers teach each other. Teaming defeats the isolation that is a prime cause of teacher alienation and burn-out. Essentially, for the same reason that people tell jokes or prompted you to read this book, we are inquisitive, voyeuristic animals who depend on checking out how other people think and interpret our world. Teaming embraces the totality of life. New people. New perspectives. New skill base development. New life opportunities.

In your effort to search for a partner, you pursue formal and informal routes. Formally, you make an announcement at a staff meeting. You had previously made a personal vow to stay quiet at staff meetings, so when you do speak up, people are stunned to hear your voice. You choose your words carefully to avoid sounding self-glorifying, which is the death knell of team development. "As most of you know, I have started a lunchtime school club," you begin. "Inclusion is our goal. If any other staff member would like to drop by, we would love to see you and partner with you. Thanks."

You realize that your message would have gone over better if students from the club had made that announcement. If you could do it again, you would have students come to the staff meeting to ask for additional adult help. You now have something to consider for the next staff meeting.

Informally, you search for a team partner by reaching out to your friends on the staff. Your sales pitch is honest, factual, open, and realistic. When you walk up to a colleague, you are frank when you describe the time investment you think the club will demand. You are open about the benefits and the pitfalls of what you are trying to accomplish. Most of all, you emphasize how much fun it will be to share in this experience. You leave these hallway conversations more optimistic than ever before, because the more you articulate your vision for the club, the more the whole concept slides into focus. What you are really doing is solidifying your sales pitch through practice. Also, by talking up the club so much, you are even increasing your own enthusiasm.

After all of your efforts, you come back to one essential truth. Expect nothing. If someone does express interest in collaboration and seems willing to give up his or her own free-time, fantastic! Other staff members' reticence is not a slam on you. People are busy. Over the years, you will find that there will be an ebb and a flow of staff involvement in your club. The more positive you are, the more likely it is that positive things will happen to you.

➜ WHAT STRATEGY WILL YOU TRY NEXT?—P. 130

Option 3. Plan Your Ideal Community Service Club

WOW, this is depressing. You find yourself sitting alone in your classroom. Even the "Welcome" sign you taped to your front door is starting to droop. You did everything you could to promote your idea, but it got no traction. This is the moment when you need to self-reflect. A novice would take this apathy toward community outreach as a personal slam. You know better. People are busy. But you still haven't yet sold your concept to your school community.

Don't give up. This is your reset button. How can you re-launch? Abraham Lincoln said, "Success is going from failure to failure without losing your enthusiasm." The more energized you are, the more your club will thrive. You realize that your challenge right now is to remain patient and remain mindful of what it is you want to accomplish.

You now have twenty minutes of uninterrupted time to re-think your school club plan. For the club to be successful, you need to plan backward not forward. You imagine you are at a PTA meeting five years from now celebrating the success of your landmark club. In your imaginary scenario, your PTA question-and-answer period starts off with a softball question tossed at you by the PTA president: "For a beginning teacher, or for any teacher for that matter, you have done a remarkable job. Above and beyond your contractual duties, you have started the most dynamic club our school has seen in a long, long, time. What were the steps that led to where your club is now?"

You have heard it over and over again, that any club takes three to five years to fully mature. During your presentation to the PTA, you outline how your club functions in the following categories:

- ▸ Purpose
- ▸ Student composition
- ▸ Predictable routine
- ▸ Impact on the school and community involvement
- ▸ Fiscal viability

Because clubs can take many forms, your decide to model your fledgling group after one of your colleague's ideas—The Mensch Club. The Merriam Webster Dictionary defines "mensch" as a person of integrity and honor. In any organization, 1 percent of the people cause over 80 percent of the grief. At your school of 1,000 students, the task of creating a list of the twenty most intolerable and intolerant students is quite easy. The original idea for the group was to embrace and give a home to the most academically at-risk students, the social troublemakers, and the wayward souls. The goal was to help turn them around through positive role modeling, camaraderie, and inclusion.

Considering how programmed we are to be social animals, your group's vitality depends upon how it is perceived by the wider school community. You don't want to negatively label these students. You don't want to create the Perpetrator Club. So your purpose needs to be re-evaluated.

Purpose: If your goal is to create an environment where students are more committed to the well being of the whole school community, you need to include the whole school community in the process. In essence, your wider purpose is *to redirect your wayward students toward becoming effective, service minded leaders.*

Student composition: Since you are well aware of Labeling Theory, you are carefule to pursue a wide spectrum of student participants. Essentially, you want to avoid tracking students. In her Feb 25, 2000 article, "Keeping Track, Part 1: The Policy and Practice Of Curriculum Inequality," Jeannie Oaks asserts that, "Analyses of how tracking affects the day-to-day school experiences of young people support the argument that such basic elements of schooling can prevent rather than promote educational goals."

Tracking even affects school clubs. Hence, while the focus of your club is to provide a safe place for students away from the drama inherent in school life, including only the high maintenance students will lead to the demise of your beautiful intentions.

But there are two angles on this. If you want to embrace a rainbow of students, you will need to attract high achieving as well as struggling students. The best way to do this is through communal action. With a directed purpose focused on service-learning, you can bring in students from every subset of the school.

The obligation is on you to walk the walk of inclusivity. Every kid who walks in through the door needs to be welcomed and given a purpose. Predictable routines and structure are vital to fostering extensive student participation.

Predictable routine: One of the best things a routine can do is help with transitions. There are more icebreakers than school days. When students show up you can start with a creative question— "Aside from super speed, super strength, being able to fly or being invisible, which superpower would you like to have?" These type of questions can give you beautiful insights into how your students really think.

Once the club's meeting starts, relying on Roberts Rules of Order may solidify your participants' expectations. This will create a safer environment for them to come back to. Each one of your projects follows the same trajectory:

- ▸ Survey the community or target audience to localize the need.
- ▸ Brainstorm viable actions for their service project.
- ▸ Advertise. The more the better. Your club's goal is to unify community through meaningful action. The better your club promotes and publicizes its work the more social gravitas you have and the more students will want to be involved. Follow through. Your team will need to complete the goal of its service-learning project. Publicize the outcome. Your goal is to keep the positive vibe going. Success breeds more success.
- ▸ Reflection. Did your team fully realize the goal of their work? Developing the habits of mind to continually learn from past endeavors is one of the best life lessons any teacher can confer on students.

With minimal guidance, the students will want to set up their own routines and traditions. The more students set up the club, the more vibrant the club will be. Your job is to coach them along to pursue being inclusive and to follow through on their best intentions. Quite often, being a coach also means allowing students to fail. Ideally, after multiple iterations, you will find a pattern at to which projects your students are interested in pursuing year after year. While yearly traditional projects can add stability to your club, make a conscious effort not to limit yourself with an overly predictable year-to-year pattern. You have welcomed students to own their community involvement based on terms they have created.

Impact on the school and community involvement: To nurture your club's ongoing success it needs to be about something. There is a limited shelf life for any party where people just sit around and talk about their problems. Your goal is to avoid the detrimental effects of labeling, as outlined in Option One of this chapter. The key to sustaining your group is service and fun. People want to derive a sense of purpose from what they do. According to the National Service-Learning Clearinghouse, America's most comprehensive service-learning resource, there is a long list of benefits to involving youth in community service. "Young people gain access to the range of supports and opportunities (or developmental assets) they need to grow up healthy, caring, and responsible. One study of youth civic activism found multiple benefits in cultivating youth and community involvement (Lewis-Charpetal., 2003). These benefits include:

- Increased sense of self-efficacy as young people learn that they can impact real social challenges, problems, and needs.
- Higher academic achievement and interest in furthering their education.
- Enhanced problem-solving skills, ability to work in teams, and planning abilities.
- Enhanced civic engagement attitudes, skills and behaviors. Many leaders in public service today speak about how they were nurtured, inspired, and shaped in early experiences in community service or volunteering.[5]

The essence of your Web search is that schools need to widen their missions to include more than academic measures of growth. Your club will nurture academic success by enabling students to experience the wider application of academic study by witnessing its implementation in a practical, community-building setting.

Fiscal viability: You will be amazed at how much your community and extended community will want to help you. Within your community, you need to keep in mind the refrain, "You can't say you can't play." Your school club, by its very nature, needs to be inclusive to thrive. Hence, you consciously stay away from any perception that group members need to pay to join. Taking up a collection will surely backfire. Any money coming in will need to come from four sources: your pocket (least desirable); fundraisers (possible, but requiring a lot of front-end work); inside your community support agencies (PTA, School Site Council, boosters, generous sugar daddy benefactors); and outside your community support agencies. Local community service clubs like the Rotary Club or Lions Club are aching to help bring out the best in students.

Just typing in the key words, "grants for school clubs," produces eleven million hits. The money is out there. The challenge lies in creating the time to access it. This is part of the reason your club may need three to five years to be fully vibrant. Before you start to pursue grants, you will need to have a complete idea of the direction in which your club is heading. The pressure from grant applications to articulate your plan in writing will help solidify your vision.

Supporting schools represents a great public relations opportunity for hundreds of companies and foundations. Writing up a grant is a far less intimidating task than it might seem. The questions within any grant will center around several categories: (1) demographics of your school, (2) club agenda, (3) academic standards the club's projects will address, (4) why the club is essential to your academic program, (5) costs embedded within running your club. When you write up the grant, just follow best essay writing practices. Steal from the questions. Eliminate all of your whys. To insure that your grant will be funded, mind the due dates for the grant, and make sure one of your most capable writing colleagues takes a look at your final write-up before you hit "send." A fantastic bonus of writing out your ideas is that you can simply resend this uniform write-up to multiple foundations—instead of tackling each grant separately and having to recreate the wheel over and over again.

In your fantasy, the PTA uses your format for a socially responsible club as a model for all future school endeavors.

As your lunchtime brainstorm comes to an end, you are more and more appreciative of the ripple effect you can have by seeing your ideals through to a tangible reality. Now your goal is to get to work so students can bring out the best in your community.

→ WHAT STRATEGY WILL YOU TRY NEXT?—P. 130

---

5 Chung, 1997; Coe-Regan et al, in press; Lewis-Charp et al., 2003; Tannenbaum, S. C., 2007; and YMCA of the USA, 2004. http://www.servicelearning.org/instant_info/fact_sheets/cb_facts/benefits-community-based-service-learning

Option 4. Foster Student Leadership

THE list of benefits to be derived from organizing a school club begins and ends with fostering student leadership. Creating an environment in which students take active control over their own lives and interests is an essential step toward fortifying the leaders of tomorrow. The beauty of a school club is that it provides fertile ground for students to experiment with leadership roles with limited or no pressure. Your goal as the club's mentor is to bring out the best in all of your students.

How can you bring out the best in your fledgling student leaders? You find that side conversations work best. After your group has its own internal elections, you decide to have a weekly board meeting. This is the time for the leadership of your club to make collective decisions about the direction your wider membership will be embarking on. This pre-general meeting planning time is an ideal opportunity to create unified direction and camaraderie.

After getting the system started, you make the best decision of all. You let the group fail. As your leadership research points out, students need to learn how "to be creative and take initiative" (Riggio 2009). The capacity for resilience is one of the best tools a child can gain. Not every one of your group's projects will succeed. We all often learn more from failure than from success. With your watchful eye and calm inaction, you give the solid message to students that you are aware of what they are doing and you trust that they will make good choices.

Throughout, you keep in mind that school is the place to learn new skills; school is not the place to merely show off what you know.

Students will continue to thrive and grow when you give them the space to flourish.

→ WHAT STRATEGY WILL YOU TRY NEXT?—P. 130

Option 5. Nurture New Ideas without Dominating Students

WITHIN the life of any endeavor there will be highs and lows. Because you already know how to bring out the best in beginning leadership, a question still remains: what should you do when there are apparently no student leaders?

Before you back out of the picture and put on your coach/monitor hat, you need to set the playing field. Every kid has something to share and an idea of what they want out of the club. Fostering collective student ownership of their own club is the key to your club's on-going success.

You decide to follow the same format with students now as you did solo during your lunch hour. You will show students how to imagine the club they want and then deconstruct backward to the present. Ultimately, this backwards planning exercise could get them to achieve the club they envision. With a slew of markers and sheets of butcher paper, you await club members. You have a different topic written on each piece of butcher paper:

- ▶ Purpose
- ▶ Student composition
- ▶ Predictable routine
- ▶ Impact on the school and community involvement
- ▶ Fiscal viability

You roll out only one paper at a time for the group to discuss and process.

When students enter, you tell them your plan. This activity is a way for students to reflect about each one of your prompts and the wider implications. In addition, students open themselves to their peers' perspectives in a self-directed, exploratory manner.

It is wise to break the lesson into three different segments:

Stage 1: Students walk around the classroom and respond to the prompt on the chart paper. The less talking there is during this step, the better, as your focus is on self-reflection. You urge students to write only their own ideas and initial their comments.

Stage 2: On the second pass, students write responses to their peers' initial prompts. The paper has the look of an illuminated manuscript radiating out from the initial query in the middle of the page.

Stage 3: You have students team up with a friend and move about the room, discussing their own and other students' responses to the prompt. The more you are involved in these rolling conversations, the more insights you will gain about how students really think and the more students will take the task seriously.

You see that this lesson simultaneously promotes dialogue and checks for understanding around each one of the core elements of your burgeoning club. The added bonus is that the chart paper products created now can easily be used as reference guides for end-of-year reflections.

After students leave and you are cleaning up at the end of lunch, you take a moment to finally read what they wrote. Thank goodness they put their initials under what they contributed. You immediately gain new insights about what students hope to get out of your club.

Just like a veteran teacher you look at this lesson and you think of ways you can improve it or make it more your own. Your first consideration is to make sure to balance time between quiet reflection and social engagement.

➜ WHAT STRATEGY WILL YOU TRY NEXT?—P. 130

13. Presenting at a Conference

"**I LOVED** your lesson today," one of your colleagues says, smiling through a mouthful of tuna sandwich. "You should really share your ideas. They're solid."

Your back and shoulders roll back a little bit with confidence. "Really? I feel as though I'm constantly making things up as I go along."

"That is the essence of being a professional in anything," the veteran teacher responds. "Every professional I have ever met, in any field, has a vision for what they want to accomplish. The real challenge is flexibility and responsiveness to changing demands along the way to your end goal. The beauty of what you do is your responsiveness. I know a lot of teachers who could benefit from learning how you run your classroom. Have you ever thought about presenting at a conference?"

"No. I'm too busy just getting by right now," you respond quickly, but after lunch, your mind starts reeling with questions:

- ▸ How would I even manage to present at a conference?
- ▸ What is the process? Do I need to apply? What do I need to submit and to whom?
- ▸ What are the costs involved?
- ▸ How much do I need to prepare?
- ▸ What if I make a total fool of myself or, worse, fail?

That afternoon as you start to head home, you begin thinking of possibilities. A large part of you likes a challenge. Maybe presenting at a conference is a challenge worth embracing. It may still be early in your teaching career, but it is always the right time to take a professional risk.

There are numerous reasons adults attend conferences: getting away; connecting with old friends; the rejuvenating strength of being involved with a professional guild, and, first and foremost, the desire to learn and grow. People of all ages and backgrounds want to thrive.

That night, you give yourself twenty minutes to search for conference possibilities. You find that opportunities abound for anyone who is looking. Teacher associations are highly motivated to bring in new blood. There are three main cores of professional organizations: information exchange, political advocacy, and skill enhancement for its members.

Beyond local, state, and national unions, you discover content-specific associations at the local, state, and national levels. Social studies, English, foreign languages, physical education, music, and more all have their own advocacy groups. There are also state grade-level associations from the League of Elementary Schools, League of Middle Schools and League of High Schools. For each website you discover, your confidence grows that your constructive contributions will be welcome.

Ten minutes into your search for the right fit of an association to pursue, your mind rollercoasters through possibilities of what you can do. Your major obstacle is time. To do anything well, you want to invest the time to fulfill your goal completely. To keep your presentation feasible in terms of time preparation, you decide to focus on one of your many successful units.

Starting your life as a presenter follows the same format as your blossoming teaching career. You see this as a matching game between your skill base and interests and the goals of the association you want to affiliate with. Once you start with backward planning, your presentation of what you do in your classroom seems to write itself. Most presentation time slots last only forty-five minutes to an hour. Some associations are more focused on panel discussions. There are many possibilities.

Applying to present is much easier than you initially thought. Using the online registration page, you enter your basic information—name, school, contact information, and so on. The most difficult part is writing an abstract of what you intend to present. A wise move is to ask conference organizers for a model to help you frame your writing. Your end product comes into view. You start to imagine yourself being there. Almost as quickly, you start to see yourself looking at your credit card bill for the trip. You can feel the thud as your aspirations hit the financial brick wall of reality.

The next day, you broach the topic of presenting at a conference to your colleague who first made the suggestion. "You got my mind thinking of possibilities. Last night, I found a good fit for an association that I would like to be more involved with. I even came up with a cool idea for a presentation. Before I could hit the send button, reality hit. How can I afford to go? There are membership fees and travel costs. What if I'm scheduled to present on a Friday? I don't have substitute days to spare. I'm interested, but not now. Maybe later."

Your teaching partner brushes away your dismayed look with a small shake of his head. "If you don't act now, when will you? Life is filled with excuses. Developing involvement in a professional organization completes your repertoire as a professional educator. Presenting at a conference gives you an ideal venue to nurture another aspect of your professional life. You have more insights and ideas to share than you realize. More people want to help you than you realize.

"Did you talk to anyone at the district office yet? There may be money there to help you. How about the organization you want to present at? Often, there are grants to help beginning teachers with travel expenses. The worst anyone will say is 'no,' and then you are back to where you started. You really have nothing to lose."

With the deadline to submit the application to present still a few weeks away, you have time to pursue financial help. Nothing beats face-to-face contact. Your first step is to talk with your principal. After a few telephone calls to the district office on your behalf, you follow through with an afternoon at the district headquarters. Because this is your first conference, you are given a stipend to present at the conference. All you need to do is complete a post-conference write-up for the school district's records.

Believe it or not, you are on your way. Even if you think you will be embarrassed, people want to celebrate you. Well ahead of the conference, you make a point to tell friends and family what you are doing. Relishing other people's joy in your accomplishments is part of the fun of your new adventure.

Now, how do you choose to best prepare for this moment so you can continue to shine? You:

1. Prepare for the presentation—p. 141
2. Deal with an empty room or people walking out on you—p. 142
3. Adjust to the unexpected—p. 142
4. Find everything goes perfectly—p. 143
5. Improvise your presentation at the last minute—p. 144
6. Deal with a heckler—p. 145

Following is a discussion of each option. You can move from one to the next, or you can jump between options at any time.

Option 1. Prepare for the Presentation

TENNIS legend Arthur Ashe once said, "One important key to success is self-confidence. An important key to self-confidence is preparation." You keep this in mind as you prepare your presentation.

You have arrived at the conference hotel and checked into your room. Your first stop in the hotel is the breakout room where your session will be taking place. Just as you did when setting up your classroom, you take a moment to get a sense of the room. It is a long rectangular room with two doors on one side and a white board at the head of the room.

You look at the entry doors. This is where your audience will get their first impression of you. You want to set up your visuals for maximum impact on the audience. Never taking anything for granted, you packed your own painter's tape to hang posters. You also managed to borrow a portable LCD projector from your school district along with extension cords. Now that you have the room to yourself, you invest ten minutes in figuring out where you should set up your visuals, posters, and your computer and projector.

Next, you look at the room's seating arrangement. You remind yourself that you will probably have only a handful of minutes to re-create this layout. Another presenter will be finishing up using the room only a few minutes before you will be on stage, and the seating may have been moved for that session. Whatever you have in mind for any room reconfiguring it will have to be expedient, fluid, and easy to do.

You know that your seating layout should support your goal for an interactive session. You will need walkways so you have access to the entire room. One of the best ways to lose your audience is to stand in one place throughout a forty-five-minute session.

Taking this time to manipulate the space is vital for your state of mind. Sitting in an audience chair, you start to visualize your presentation. Several aspects become clear: there will be time pressures and room management issues.

During your presentation, you need to be aware of your pacing. Move too quickly, and you will have to repeat yourself for clarity. Move too slowly, and some attendees will walk out to find what they think might be a better session. Most likely, you will also have to leave time at the end of your session to hand out an evaluation sheet.

In terms of room management, you will have to tolerate late-comers and early-leavers. Unlike your classroom, there is always the possibility of a fluid movement of attendees traipsing in and out of your session, creating a flittering distraction in your peripheral vision. You never know who knows who or what the full story is about any member of your audience. Therefore your only choice is to be polite, focus on your presentation, and not waste time trying to control your audience. Allow the quality of your presentation to captivate and motivate your audience to stay attuned.

You do a quick walk-through of your presentation. Keeping in mind your planned placement for visuals and seat arrangement, you talk through what you plan to say to a (hopefully) packed house. The fifteen minutes you spend here will be vital in you being able to present a professional presentation tomorrow.

Walking out of your presentation room filled with the confidence that only preparation can bring, you turn your attention to the other elements of the conference. Your breakout session is a minor speck in the larger conference universe. You may want to look into some political advocacy working groups, get some free memorabilia from corporate sponsors' displays in the central exhibit hall, develop networking opportunities, or just hang out and make new friends. Feeling refreshed, you set out to explore.

➔ HOW DO YOU HANDLE THINGS NEXT?—P. 140

Option 2. Deal With an Empty Room or People Walking Out On You

TEN minutes into your presentation, you start to question yourself, as half of the six people who have shown up to your breakout session walk out.

Rattled is an understatement. The remaining audience members' eyes are filled with pity. What is happening? Is the content uninteresting ? Or is it your presentation style?

As you muddle through what remains of your presentation, you try to squelch your disillusionment. The truth is that what you *have* done is remarkable. You have embraced life and taken a risk. You put yourself out there instead of resigning your life's ambition to being comfortable. This is your first attempt. Failure is a beautiful motivator in your persistent quest to do better.

Looking at the bigger picture helps. Quite possibly, your breakout session was the second choice for numerous other potential attendees. You will never know. Instead of getting caught up in a useless pity party, you laugh this off. What can you learn from this? What may seem a catastrophic event to you is really just a blip on the radar to other people.

As you walk out of your session with all of your materials in hand, you take a moment to sit down in the lounge. Reading over the evaluations from your three audience members helps give you perspective. You really did do all right. There is more to this conference than just your forty-five minutes on stage. How can you capitalize on this moment in your life to embrace being here?

Years from now, after a litany of other successes, you will have a great story to tell of your stumbling beginnings.

➜ HOW DO YOU HANDLE THINGS NEXT?—P. 140

Option 3. Adjust to the Unexpected

YOU have planned your afternoon perfectly. You will attend the session that precedes yours so you will not lose time moving from a different session to yours. The presenter appears to be in full stride. You glance at the clock on the wall and see that this is the moment that the session should be wrapping up. Apparently, you are the only one who is watching the clock. Everyone else in the room seems to be eagerly engaged in a dynamic, energized discussion. This discussion has now edged five minutes into your presentation time. You look out the door and see people pause and look in the room and then keep on walking. "Those are people who were going to attend my session and now can't!" you think to yourself.

You are in a quandary. Part of you wants to stand up and politely yell, "Hey, wrap it up. This is my time." However, you decide to play it cool and wait. By the time the presenter who went over time is done apologizing, and the participants from her session leave the room, you realize you only have half your allotted time left.

You try to model the flexibility you admire most in your veteran colleagues. Whatever your content is, you should really have no more than five key ideas. The rest of your session should be spent elaborating and massaging those ideas. If you are pressured on time, all you need to do is adjust the amount of time you devote to each idea. Instead of devoting ten minutes to flesh out each of your talking points, you will now have five. You will still cover all of your talking points. Most important, you will not complain. After all, thinking on your feet is half of the fun of being alive.

➜ HOW DO YOU HANDLE THINGS NEXT?—P. 140

Option 4. Everything Goes Perfectly— and How to Pack the Room

APPARENTLY, your session blurb grabbed more attention than you anticipated. Your session is now overly full, which reinforces your belief that your topic is controversial. You had hoped it would be. Standing in the front of the room, you reflect that the effectiveness of your presentation will be directly proportional to your preparation time. To set your presentation apart from others (which usually involve long PowerPoint® presentations), you decided to create the most innovative presentation possible, and you made a large time investment—ten hours of practice—in preparing.

Your interactive lesson has a beautiful story arc. Following the simple layout of a seven-step lesson plan, you take your audience through the setup of your idea, through implementation and importance, and end up with independent practice. Specifically, you follow an outline based on the work of Madeline Hunter (1994):

- ▸ Objectives
- ▸ Standards
- ▸ Anticipatory set
- ▸ Teaching (input, modeling, checking for understanding)
- ▸ Guided practice/monitoring
- ▸ Closure
- ▸ Independent practice

You start by presenting the problem you aim to solve. Demonstrating a historical knowledge of your topic solidifies your standing as a burgeoning expert in your field. You then outline the content of your work in your field and the objectives of your presentation. What makes your presentation unique is that you give your participants time to practice the skills you have your students work on in your classroom. You monitor and guide your participants through discussion and practical implementation of your ideas. Your PowerPoint® serves only as a backdrop to outline and guide your presentation.

During your session, you focus on body language. You want to face the audience just as you would teach a class. Simultaneously, you continually read your audience members' body language to monitor their engagement. Just as you would manage your classroom, you work the room. When an attendee appears to be more interested in his phone than your presentation, you glide over and continue your talk to the group while standing next to the distracted participant. You let your body language concentrate the audience's attention on your content.

Most important, you are accessible afterward. Doing your part to create and foster a supportive professional community is one of your primary objectives for being at the conference. Ultimately, personal relationships trump all else.

➡ HOW DO YOU HANDLE THINGS NEXT?—P. 140

Option 5. Improvise Your Presentation at the Last Minute

YOUR flexibility, resiliency, and ability to keep a cool head will be tested over and over again throughout your weekend. Unfortunately, your drive to do everything right causes you to stumble out of the gate. Now is not the time to doubt your ability to shine through. Now is the time to figure out creative solutions.

Your session is about to start. You swear you put your handouts right here.

Breathe. Yes, you need these handouts for your session. The last thing you want to project is disorganization. You take pride in being organized. Organization and congeniality are two requisite skills of being a teacher. And at this moment in time, you are not organized.

Your session is about to start. People are gathering outside the conference room door.

You suddenly realize that you don't need any handouts to complete your presentation. With time running out, you focus on the core elements of your content:

What is the short thirty-second explanation of the idea behind your presentation?

What are the global themes your presentation touches on?

How will the content of your presentation play out in other teachers' classrooms?

What are the obstacles for implementing your idea?

Why does your idea help nurture student growth?

These are all key questions you can center on in your presentation. Expounding on and personalizing these themes can be your core mission.

You step into the hotel hallway with the meeting room's door open behind you. You stand where you can see all of your participants and walk up to any one of them in three strides. "Welcome to my session," you say. "My goal is to model the hands-on pedagogy that I will be talking about." You realize that even the best managers learn to fake leadership when they need to.

The most important thing is that you work the room. You talk through your lesson idea to your participants. This gets easier the more you do it.

→ HOW DO YOU HANDLE THINGS NEXT?—P. 140

Option 6. Deal with a Heckler

IN the middle of your session, an audience member interrupts you. "Really?" you think to yourself, as you grind your teeth. Doesn't he realize that this is *your* presentation and not his? Ignoring him seems to be the best initial reaction. You continue with your talking points, because your show must go on.

Soon, your unwelcome guest interrupts again, so you decide to counter his intentional act. Because you never know someone else's story and you don't know who talks to whom behind closed doors, you place a huge priority on personal dignity. You have a responsibility to the rest of the people in the audience to model respect, and your top priority is to complete your presentation. You now have a few choices:

1. Walk over and ask the rude audience member to leave.
2. From the front of the room, single out the heckler and ask him to leave.
3. Make fun of him.
4. Ignore him.

The first two options have two potential outcomes—confrontation or compliance. Chances are, if the heckler is acting intentionally, you have a confrontation on your hands. You don't have the luxury of time to devote to staring someone down. Also, do you want to be known conference-wide as confrontational?

The third option is intriguing and daring but has the most potential to backfire. When you fight fire with fire, you will probably get you burned. This is a gamble. What you are really doing is waving a red flag in front of a bull. Is this what you want? Taking the time to engage this self-centered attention hound will only take time away from the pacing of your presentation. Still, this option can be very entertaining if you play it right.

Ignoring him is the most logical option. Because the audience will side with you, the heckler will probably stop.

You realize that there is a fifth option—laugh with him. Ultimately you are at the conference to build connections and community. Staying focused on the larger purpose bolsters your pride and commitment to rise above juvenile antics. In response to his last interruption, you calmly retort, "That is a great line. I'm going to use that later. Thank you for sharing." Another way to diffuse the situation is to compliment the heckler: "You're right. I never thought of what I just presented in that way. If you can stick around after I'm done up here, maybe we can talk that over."

You feel revitalized after your presentation; you continued to cover your information and did not fall victim to a confrontation.

→ HOW DO YOU HANDLE THINGS NEXT?—P. 140

146

14. Ending the School Year

THERE was never any doubt you would finish the school year well. Yes, some of your lessons tanked. Yes, you had some embarrassing public gaffes within your classroom and with other staff members. Nobody is perfect. But more than anything else, you completed your year with dignity. State testing is over, as well as your last major assignment. Your backward planning enabled you to collect all of your students' work and grade it in time to enter your final grades early. That is no small feat.

Ten long months. People don't realize that the average teacher works just as hard in ten months as most people work in eighteen months. Just counting up the hours—official work time and unofficial work time, when you are still thinking about work—is exhausting. After all of the exams, long nights grading homework, parent contacts, and making lesson plans, you are left with one last hurdle. How do you end the year right? How do you help students with the drive to continue the work you did with them throughout the year? Essentially, how do you nurture the seed of hope you have installed in so many students so it can flower without you?

As your school year is winding down, there is only one week left of instruction. You have managed to squeak out enough time for review and late work. In the middle of one of your last lessons, Mike raises his hand. "What are we doing for the end of the school year? Can we have a party?" A chorus of "Yeahs" erupts throughout your room.

You stand there and wait patiently. More quickly than it started, the disruption ends. "They really do respect me," you think to yourself. "I don't know yet, Mike. I need to think about it. I'll get back to you tomorrow." Wow, you are on a roll of quality right now. You didn't immediately commit to something you weren't completely sure of.

Casually, you ask around—how do the colleagues that you respect the most end their school year? You get a mixed bag of reactions, but there is one solid continual message—all teachers end the school year in the same way they ran their classrooms during the school year. You find that there is a multitude of ways teachers close out the year, from field trips beyond school, to field days within school, to low-level parties, to doing nothing.

The teachers who put paramount importance on academics throughout the year end with an academic focus; either the teacher teaches up to the end or gives up and lets students hang out for the last few days of school, because they have "earned down time."

For the teachers who put building community first, closing out the school year revolves around opportunities for closure. Devoting public and private reflection time over the last few days plays a more central role for these teachers.

Which of these plans is best for you?

What is your plan for ending your school year and making them excited to come back? You:

1. Hold end-of-year awards—p. 148
2. Allow time for class reflection—p. 151
3. Pass out letters—p. 151
4. Have students clean the classroom—p. 153
5. Have students create the foundation for next year—p. 153
6. Let students hang out—p. 154

Following is a discussion of each option. You can move from one to the next, or you can jump between options at any time.

Option 1. Hold End-of-Year Awards

A RESPECTED colleague suggests a great idea for the end of the year: student awards. "I take the end of the school year as a time to celebrate each and every child," she says. "By forcing me to focus on each student's success, my class's end-of-the-year celebration is as much for me as it is for my students."

She shows you the form that lists twenty-five awards: "Because each award is presented to both a male and female student, I make sure every kid is recognized and celebrated at least once."

You look at the categories listed on the form, "End-of-Year Awards." You are amazed by the diversity of options in the list.

End-of-Year Awards

Appearances:

	Male	Female
1. Don't I look fabulous? Best Hairstyle Award	_____	_____
2. I can see into your soul: Nicest Eyes Award	_____	_____
3. You can see my smile in the dark: Most Radiant Smile Award	_____	_____

Talents:

4. Da Vinci has nothing on me: Best Artist Award	_____	_____
5. I'll never let you down: Most Responsible Award	_____	_____
6. The glass is always full: Most Optimistic Award	_____	_____
7. These two monkeys were talking one day: Best Comedian Award	_____	_____
8. No I promise, this time I won't tell anybody: Biggest Mouth Award *(Choose students who can take a joke.)*	_____	_____
9. American Idol is waiting for me: Best Singer Award	_____	_____

10. I've got the moves:

    Best Dancer Award   _____   _____

11. It's okay that you ran over my pet squirrel:

    Sweetest Person Award   _____   _____

12. Only organic for me, dude:

    Most Consistent at Living

    a Healthy Life Award   _____   _____

13. No really, I'm laughing with you, not at you, this time:

    Likes to Laugh Award   _____   _____

14. I know I left that $100 around here somewhere:

    Most Organized Award   _____   _____

15. Macbeth gets so much better after you've read it ten times:

    Most Well-Read Award   _____   _____

16. The devil is in the details:

    Best Writer Award   _____   _____

17. There is always room for you to join us:

    Best Team Player—

    Most Inclusive Award   _____   _____

Futures:

18. Comeback player of the year:

    Most Improved Award   _____   _____

19. Daydreaming of a better world:

    Ponyboy Big Thinker

    Daydreamer Award   _____   _____

20. My life is one drama after another:

    Most Likely to End Up

    in a Soap Opera Award   _____   _____

21. How do I make *money*?

    Most Likely to be the

    next Bill Gates Award   _____   _____

22. Enough with Middle School. Bring on Graduate School!

    Genius Award

    _____   _____

23. When you put it that way, I agree the main character deserved to die:

    Most Insightful During Class Discussions

    (Future Lawyer) Award

    _____   _____

24. I told them I should have been in charge:

    Most Likely to Become President

    of the United States Award

    _____   _____

25. Can't we all just get along?

    Most Empathic,

    Nobel Peace Prize Award

    _____   _____

"It is quite simple," your colleague smiles. "Because we all teach six classes, I make six master copies. At the bottom of each master copy, I include a class list for easy reference. One week before the last day of school, I give each student a voting sheet for his or her class. I have a separate awards ceremony for each class. There are plenty of students who finish their last few assignments early, so I always have a core of students who tabulate the ballots. To save paper, I print out two awards on one sheet. The preparatory work for this takes less than half an hour of my time.

"The last day is a celebration in my classroom. Quite often I have a student act as the Master or Mistress of Ceremonies, and I just sit back and enjoy the moment. When a student is named the winner, he or she comes up to accept the award. Students often give speeches. One year, a student actually brought in a recording from the Oscars to play to wrap up the speeches. For the dancing and singing awards, students frequently perform."

"I love ending my school year this way," she concludes. "It reminds me that there is so much more to school than just work. For me nurturing the entire kid is a non-negotiable. The end-of-year awards are a small way I can help students feel appreciated."

You love the idea, but you are still curious about what other alternatives for ending the school year.

➜ WHAT PLAN WILL YOU TRY NEXT?—P. 147

Option 2. Allow Time for Class Reflection

YOU ask another respected colleague how he wraps up his school year.

"I am always interested in improving what I do," he says. "After my room is all cleaned up, I set up students' chairs in a circle. I always say the same thing to start the conversation: 'My grades are already put in, and I won't change any of my comments. I am always interested in improving my practice. Also, confession is good for the soul. What are some things you think you got away with this year that you think I don't know about?'"

Your colleague starts to laugh out loud. "Sometimes, I learn more in this ten-minute conversation than I ever wanted to know. Often it is students revealing they got away with chewing gum or arranged to meet in the bathroom and hang out there. It is always benign stuff, but I learn things that I am usually oblivious to. Texting under the desk is big right now. One kid told me she had a twenty-minute texting conversation with her friend during one of my lectures.

"One seventh grader talked about a time when he was four years old and took a cookie without permission. When I reminded him that I was only referring to events that happened during my class time, he said, straight-faced, 'I just had to tell somebody.' The entire class busted out laughing.

"So I guess you can say, I end the school year focused on giving students a clean slate, modeling forgiveness, and learning from students on how I should improve my practice."

Your stockpile of good ideas is growing.

→ WHAT PLAN WILL YOU TRY NEXT?—P. 147

Option 3. Pass Out Letters

ONE of the most important conversations you have during your inquiry has very little to do with the actual last day of school. The teacher who has had the deepest impact on your personal and professional development guides your thinking toward helping students develop long-term goals:

"My end-of-year activity actually starts midway through the school year," she says. "I ask students to brainstorm their lifelong dream, their goals for their next five years, and their immediate ambitions for this school year. Specifically, each student takes one sheet of paper and folds it into three sections. This lesson takes a full class period, but it is well worth it.

"For my instructions, I simply say, 'Dream big. Please don't worry about correct spelling or complete sentences. Just write. For the next two minutes, don't stop writing, even if you just end up writing 'I don't know what to write.' Please fill in the top third of your paper with everything you want to accomplish in your lifetime. Do you want to travel? Is community service in your future? When you are older, would you like to have a spouse and start a family? Inventions? Do you want to start a business? Will you pursue riches, fame, solitude, simplicity, or anything in between? On your mark. Get set. Go!'

"What is most important, in my opinion, is that I let my students be. I spend the next two minutes modeling attentiveness by creating my own list on the board. I may walk around to check for understanding before I start writing, but overall, I stay out of the way.

"At the end of two minutes, I challenge my students with this prompt: 'Dreaming about our future takes place on many levels. Thinking about our future is the first level. Once we write our idea out on paper, that is another level up, as our idea is there winking back at us. But putting it out there for all to hear is quite another level. Once you say something in public, your idea is out there for everyone to evaluate. Does anyone have the courage to say one of their dreams out loud?'

"I have found having students verbalize their dreams is essential. Just the act of hearing oneself say an aspiration out loud gives life to one's imagination. Isn't what makes you proud of yourself at the end of the day?—to promote hope and push students to attain their goals?"

Your fellow teacher continues, "Quite often, students will share their innermost dreams. I am always fascinated by the clarity most students have about where they want to go in their lives and who they want to be. Listening to other students' aspirations often triggers more ideas throughout the classroom as well.

"I let the sharing go on for a little bit—two to three minutes—and then I bring the students back in to the task at hand. 'Now we are moving on to the middle section of your sheet of paper. For this inner third part of your paper, please do the same thing. For the next two minutes don't stop writing, even if you just write 'I don't know what to write.' Please fill in this section of your paper with everything you want to accomplish in the next five years. On your mark. Get set. Go!'

"I then follow the same format of my modeling the list making and students sharing. When we are done, I have students fill in the bottom section. 'Great job so far,' I say. 'We are two-thirds of the way done. For your last section, please fill in all of your goals for the remaining half of this school year. On your mark. Get set. Go!'

"After students share, I give them their homework assignment. 'By tomorrow, I want you to write three letters addressed to yourself based on this brainstorm activity. You can use the same first paragraph for each of your three letters. Please describe your life now: who your friends are; what home life is like; your favorite foods—anything. When you get these letters back in the future, you will love to get a glimpse of your life in the past. The rest of the content for each of your three letters will look different.

"In your first letter, please write your goals for the remaining part of this school year. For your second letter, please use your notes from the middle part of your brainstorm sheet and write your goals for the next five years. And finally, for your third letter, please write your life goals. Please put the third letter in a self-addressed envelope. I will hold on to all three of your letters and give them back to you over the next few years. To respect your privacy, I won't open a single letter. This confidential activity is for you, not me.

"I will give back your first letter on the last day of school, so you can look back to see if you met your goals. At the end of next school year—a year and a half from now—I will give back your second letter. The second letter will give you a 'to do' list for your next half decade. Finally, in five years, I will mail you the self-addressed third letter that outlines your life goals."

You are amazed with the thoughtfulness behind this activity. Simply put, this teacher has hit on quite a few vital layers of student development. By giving students a solid base—someone to help them keep their goals in sight—community is built. Most of all, trust is nurtured. Wow. Now you know why your colleague is so beloved by so many students.

➜ WHAT PLAN WILL YOU TRY NEXT?—P. 147

Option 4. Have Students Clean the Classroom

PUTTING more students to work is a goal of yours. One of your colleagues does this beautifully. You ask how she closes out her school year.

"Work them," she says. "I think closure is so necessary for students. Asking students to help your put away posters, stack chairs, and generally clean up ten months of stuff is healthy for them. Also, there is less for me to do before I need to complete my end-of- year checkout. You will be amazed how much students want to help you clean the room.

"To prepare for this, your best bet is to buy five staple removers so multiple students can work at the same time. I try to have a plan and break students into work groups. Unfortunately, I find that I end up being a traffic cop. I try to set up a part of my classroom for students to sign yearbooks and hang out when they are done with their assigned tasks. I might also put on a movie for students who are done early.

"Overall, I can't complain. I'm left with a clean classroom and students are busy."

➜ WHAT PLAN WILL YOU TRY NEXT?—P. 147

Option 5. Have Students Create the Foundation for Next Year

YOUR quest for meaningful ways to wrap up your school year continues. One of the most dynamic teachers you work with tells you about a chart-paper exercise.

"I start the last day together with my students by emphasizing the importance of reflection and investing in the broader community. Spread across my classroom are ten sheets of butcher paper. Each paper has a different month written in the middle of it. I ask students to reflect on what we did each month in terms of academic content and important lessons we did in class. To bring seriousness to this activity, I tell them I will spread out these posters during the first week of the next school year, so my incoming students can get a preview of how I teach.

To prepare for the activity, she tells you that you should have one piece of paper for every four students in your classroom. The size of the paper doesn't matter, but if you can find a larger sheet, then more students can write at once. At the center of the paper, you write the name of a month.

It is wise to break the lesson into three different segments:

Stage 1: Students walk around the classroom and respond to the prompt on the chart paper. The less students talk during this step, the better, as your focus is self-reflection. You urge students to write only their own ideas and initial their comments (five minutes).

Stage 2: On the second pass, students write responses to their peers' initial prompts. The paper has the look of an illuminated manuscript radiating out from the initial query in the middle of the page. You remind students not to talk so that they can focus on their writing (five minutes).

Stage 3: You have students team up with a friend and move about the room, discussing their own and other students' responses to the prompt. The more you are involved in these rolling conversations, the more insights you will gain about how students really think and the more students will take the task seriously.

"After students leave, and I am cleaning up at the end of the day," she concludes, "I take a moment to read what they wrote. Thank goodness they put their initials under what they contributed. I immediately gain new insights about what students got out of my class."

→ WHAT PLAN WILL YOU TRY NEXT?—P. 147

Option 6. Let Students Hang Out

ONE teacher you respect a lot because of his beautiful rapport with his students says he doesn't do anything special to end his year with students.

"Students are always told what to do and what not to do. I see the end of the school year as an opportunity for students to begin the summer early. Depending on the weather, we either have a field day or I just show a movie. Most students end up hanging out and signing yearbooks.

"The reason I like doing this is that I have the opportunity to spend individual time with each of my students. I guess you can say I close out my year one student at a time."

You like the laissez-faire attitude behind this approach. Before you can respond to his idea, he continues: "You know my approach can really bottom out. With too much open, undirected time, sometimes I need to put out last-minute drama that springs up. But I find that if I lay out my behavioral expectations at the beginning of the period, everything runs more smoothly. The last thing I want to do is to put out a social wildfire on my last day."

→ WHAT PLAN WILL YOU TRY NEXT?—P. 147

References

Bloom, Benjamin S., Max D. Engelhart, Edward J. Furst, Walter H. Hill, and David R. Krathwohl. *Taxonomy of Educational Objectives: The Classification of Educational Goals. Handbook 1: Cognitive Domain.* New York: Longman, 1956.

Joseph Campbell. *The Hero with a Thousand Faces.* Princeton: Princeton University Press, 1968.

Clark, Richard E. "Fostering the Work Motivation of Individuals and Teams." *Performance Improvement* 42, no. 3 (2003): 21–29.

Common Core State Standards Initiative. http://www.corestandards.org/.

Disability Rights. http://www.dredf.org/special_education/iep_cycle.shtml

Ervasti, Jenni, Mika Kivimäki, Riikka Puusniekka, Pauliina Luopa, Janna Pentti, Sakari Suominen, Kirsi Ahola, Jussi Vahtera, and Marianna Virtanen. "Students' School Satisfaction as Predictor of Teachers' Sickness Absence: A Prospective Cohort Study." *European Journal of Public Health* 22, no. 2 (April 2012): 215–219.

Fournier, G. (n.d.). *Locus of Control.* Retrieved from http://psychcentral.com/encyclopedia/2009/locus-of-control/

Gardner, Howard. *Frames of Mind: The Theory of Multiple Intelligences.* New York: Basic Books, 1983.

Hinton, S. E. *The Outsiders.* New York: Penguin, 1997 (first published 1967).

Howe, James. *The Misfits.* New York: Atheneum Books for Young Readers, 2003.

Hunter, Madeline. *Enhancing Teaching.* New York: Alpha Books, 1994.

Jones, Fred. *Tools for Teaching,* 2nd ed. Santa Cruz, CA: Fredric H. Jones & Associates, 2007.

Kelling, George L., and James Q. Wilson. "Broken Windows: The Police and Neighborhood Safety." *Atlantic Monthly* (March 1982): 29–38.

Krashen, Stephen. *Explorations in Language Acquisition and Use.* Portsmouth, NH: Heinemann, 2003.

Mackin, Deborah. *The Team-Building Tool Kit: Tips and Tactics for Effective Workplace Teams,* 2nd ed. New York: AMACOM, 2007.

National Dissemination Center for Children with Disabilities. "Supports, Modifications, and Accommodations for Students." September 2010. http://nichcy.org/schoolage/accommodations#part2.

New America Foundation Federal Education Budget Project. "Individuals with Disabilities Education Act Overview." March 26, 2012. http://febp.newamerica.net/background-analysis/individuals-disabilities-education-act-overview.

Ontario Ministry of Agriculture, Food and Rural Affairs. "Resolving Conflict: Factsheet." Last revised August 2006. http://www.omafra.gov.on.ca/english/rural/facts/06-067.htm#guide.

Pope, Denise Clark. *Doing School: How we are creating a generation of stressed out, materialistic, and miseducated students*. New Haven: Yale, 2001.

Putnam, Robert D. "The Prosperous Community: Social Capital and Public Life." *American Prospect* 4, no. 13 (Spring 1993): 35–42.

Rath, Tom, and Donald O. Clifton. *How Full Is Your Bucket?* New York: Gallup Press, 2004.

Riggio, Ronald E. "What 100 Years of Research Tells Us About Effective Leadership." *Cutting-Edge Leadership* (blog), *Psychology Today,* November 20, 2009. http://www.psychologytoday.com/blog/cutting-edge-leadership/200911/what-100-years-research-tells-us-about-effective-leadership.

Salem, Marc. "Learn How to Read People and Detect Lies." Marc Salem's Mind Games. 2008. http://www.marcsalem.com/tools.cfm.

Sanchez, Mark. "Facts & Statistics." Make Beats, Not Beat Downs. http://www.makebeatsnotbeatdowns.org/facts_new.html

Steinbeck, John. *The Pearl*. New York: Penguin, 1993 (first published 1947).

U.S. Department of Health and Human Services, Children's Bureau. http://www.acf.hhs.gov/programs/cb/

Willis, Janine, and Alexander Todorov. "First Impressions: Make Up Your Mind After a 100-Ms Exposure to a Face." *Psychological Science* 17, no. 7 (2006): 592–598.